FOREVER CHANGED

How a Global Pandemic Changed My Direction, My Purpose, and My Life

JOSEPH JAFFE

Copyright 2023: Joseph Jaffe

No part of this book may be reproduced in any form or by any electronic or mechanical means, including information storage and retrieval systems, without permission in writing from the author, except by a reviewer who may quote brief passages in a review.

ISBN: 979-8-9885058-9-1

TABLE OF CONTENTS

Dedication		5
Forever Changed – Foreword		6
Plan D		9
Chapter 1.	The Thing about Global Pandemics	14
Chapter 2.	Prelude to a Pandemic	21
Chapter 3.	Priorities	29
Chapter 4.	Oh Yeah, I need Open Heart Surgery	38
Chapter 5.	Do you want it Now?	47
Chapter 6.	Hello I'm Joseph Jaffe and I'm a Talk Show Host	57
Chapter 7.	Signs	68
Chapter 8.	Anatomy of a Show	79
Chapter 9.	The Business Model of Life	87
Chapter 10.	Error and Trial	101
Chapter 11.	Groundhog Day in the Metaverse	108
Chapter 12.	Take the Offer	121
Chapter 13.	Does Money Buy Happiness?	131
Chapter 14.	All In	141
Chapter 15.	A $Penny for your Soul	152
Chapter 16.	The Formula	163
Chapter 17.	Amor	173
Chapter 18.	Veritas	183
Chapter 19.	Vigor	194
Chapter 20.	Slippage	204
Chapter 21.	Blackjack	214
About the Author		226

DEDICATION

First and foremost, a message of hope, positivity and optimism, to my wife, Terri, and children, Amber, Aaron and Jack. You are my "Forever Changed" inner circle and have witnessed – or been witness to – the change firsthand. It hasn't always been pretty. The Trifecta of Trauma (COVID, Open Heart Surgery and the passing of Mom, Nat and Granny Nat) wasn't easy, but here we are. And there is only one direction. Forward.

I love you all so much and thank you for sticking with me through all this messy.

Secondly, to Mom, Nat and Granny Nat. I miss you more now than yesterday, and tomorrow I will miss you even more. Thank you for being my lifelong muse, my writer's block and cure. I hope you and Dad are enjoying the book. Please let me know if your autographed copy ever arrived. I did send it via Amazon Prime.

The cover of this book was designed by the incredible Sabet. It is not a static image, but a dynamic video. To see it in its intended magnificence, visit foreverchanged.life)

Finally, to all of you. Readers. Community Members. Humans. A group of strangers who care about each other a little more than they should and care about me a little more than you should. Keep caring. Keep sharing. Don't stop believing.

FOREVER CHANGED – FOREWORD

I MET JOSEPH JAFFE ON A WEDNESDAY MORNING AT A CONFERENCE where he was opening the day and I was scheduled to close it. As I listened to him talk about the background for his new book, I was struck by a quote and approached him after his presentation and asked him if I could borrow it for my remarks at the end of the conference. We started up a conversation and in fifteen minutes, he had not only granted me permission to use the quote but asked if I would write the forward for the book. I told him that I would be honored because it would give me the chance to share Catie's story.

Catie is our middle child of seven kids. When she was just seven years old, Catie was diagnosed with an Atypical Teratoid Rhabdoid Tumor the size of a roll of quarters in the base of her spinal column. The tumor was rare, the prognosis was poor, but the determination of her spirit and the light in her eyes gave us all hope that Catie would beat her cancer. That's where the quote from Joe comes in. *"Hope, positivity, and optimism in a time of despair."*

Joe was talking about the pandemic; I heard it as a tribute to my little girl.

No kid had ever beaten an ATRT tumor and so Hope was a scarce commodity. The only Hope for Catie was offered by St. Jude Children's Research Hospital. Catie and her mom Christine moved to Memphis, TN to undergo treatment at St. Jude and Catie underwent thirty-one radiation treatments and two rounds of stem-cell salvage and chemotherapy. Catie's infectious smile and attitude even had her doctors believing. We all believed because pediatric cancer was an acknowledged death sentence until very recently and yet there was a first kid who beat leukemia, a first kid who beat a brain tumor, a first kid who beat osteosarcoma. Every victory, every success in the battle against pediatric cancer began with that first kid, and many of those first kids were treated at St. Jude. Could Catie be one of them?

No.

Hope, positivity, and optimism in a time of despair.

Catie's diagnosis was just a preview of what despair looked like. Now the tumor was back and we knew and she knew that she was going to die. We had sixty-one days with Catie from the time we learned that the tumor was back until she died, and that seven-year-old taught us more about living in the midst of her dying than I have learned in all my years. The night we learned of the tumor coming back, Christine and I wrote in our journal, "in many ways, Catie's tumor got the best of her, but it never broke her spirit, it never took away her ability to gift any person that came into contact with her from coming away from the experience better for having spent time with her". For many of those precious sixty-one days, Catie would start the day by asking, "is today the day I am going to die?" We would honestly answer her by saying, no, today doesn't look like the day and then she would say, 'then what are we going to do today?"

A few weeks into the sixty-one days, Catie sat her mom down and said she wanted to talk about her legacy. She said that she understood that St. Jude was not able to cure her, but what about the next kid. She made us promise that we would do all we could to support the St. Jude mission of Finding Cures and Saving Children so that no child die in the dawn of life. And then Catie went deeper. She said that she wanted her legacy to be that on her eighth birthday, on April 23rd, that she pay for everything at St. Jude on that day; the treatments, the research, the salaries for doctors and nurses and for Ron the painter who kept the hallways looking fresh and wonderful for all of the kids.

Hope, positivity, and optimism in a time of despair.

Thank you for allowing me to share our daughter Catie with you. It is my hope that she inspires you to adopt an attitude of positivity and that in hearing about her, you are "Forever Changed".

As I read Forever Changed, the concept that kept resonating with me was opportunity. Opportunities are with each of us on a daily basis and yet the pandemic provided all of us with a shared, singular moment of opportunity unlike any other in history. We were all faced with similar restrictions, barriers, fears and limitations; yet some recognized the opportunity in the midst of that despair and seizing upon that opportunity grew from it. Others stayed stuck in the despair. What did you do?

The good news is that the opportunity still exists. The opportunity to embrace optimism and positivity is always with us. The opportunity to HOPE in times of despair is an opportunity that like the pandemic, we all share. I would have loved to have been present during a conversation between Joseph and Catie. In my mind I can picture the rich dialog between an admitted serial entrepreneur and a seven-year-old dying of cancer. The wisdom that would have emerged from that conversation is part of this book; continue to treat each new day as the gift that it is and make the most of it. Lean in to change, you might as well be comfortable with it, it's not going away. Believe in yourself and choose to be hopeful, positive and optimistic and be willing to allow yourself to be Forever Changed. Enjoy!

Kevin - Catie's dad

PREFACE
PLAN D

My head is swirling right now. I'm at that incredible moment that anyone who has written a book before or written something, especially after overcoming writer's block, would know.

It's almost like a euphoric state because you know you're ready to continue.

Writer's block, if you will, has plagued me since September 2022 until June 2023. I set out originally to write this book in three weeks, and I did. I actually completed it in two weeks and six days. However, for some reason, I couldn't move it forward from that moment. It was all the operational stuff, the editing, and figuring out which platform to use - to self-publish or not to self-publish – was that the question? But for whatever reason, it just didn't happen.

If I were to start this chapter, it would probably have been with these words: "I'm a failure. I'm a complete failure. I'm an utter failure. I failed miserably."

I had a bold vision to publish a book in three weeks, and here we are, almost a year later. As you're reading this, you'll notice it's out of sequence. I trust you to put the pieces together and figure it out. Life is not neat. Life is not tidy. Life is not about everything proceeding according to plan.

> *"Mann Tracht, Un Gott Lacht"*
> - old Yiddish adage translated as "Man Plans, and God Laughs."

NAVIGATING LOSS

As I reflect on 2023, I can confidently say that it was a year filled with more challenges than both 2020 and 2021 combined: COVID and heart surgery were only the beginning.

The most devastating loss came with the passing of my mother in January 2023. I had hoped I would complete this book in time to read it to her. She played such a significant role in shaping this book.

For those of you keeping score, that's Cancer 2. Humans 0.

I dedicated all 5 of my previous books to my mother (and of course my wife, kids, and even dog.) This book is more than a dedication. It's a tribute and homage. I hope, in some way, she can sense and comprehend these words, and I will strive to make her proud, even from afar.

Life moves on.

We find ourselves in 2023, and the book was back on schedule. I owe my gratitude to Kevin O'Brien, who didn't just write the foreword, he moved me forward. He never gave up on me.

Throughout the process, he remained steadfast, checking in every month or so to see how things were progressing. It was not just about seeing his foreword published; he had a genuine vested interest in me, my story, and my mother. Our conversations always began with inquiries about my mother's well-being, only to eventually discover the heartbreaking news of her passing.

His final call to me (before I wrote this) was from a different number because he suspected I was not taking his calls. I told him that this was not the case, but he was correct. I had been screening his calls, embarrassed to have to talk to him and explain that the book was still on hold.

Kevin – if you were astute enough to switch numbers, you were no doubt intuitive enough to know I was lying to you when I said I wasn't avoiding you. Thank you for persisting.

FINDING PURPOSE AMIDST CHALLENGES

The year 2023 has been a time of perseverance and pursuit.

At the time of publishing, my business talk show, Joseph Jaffe is not Famous, still has not garnered the audience and monetization I envisioned; nor has it been bought by CNBC. I am still **not** famous. Please visit www.youtube.com/josephjaffeisnotfamous or subscribe to my channel at www.bit.ly/subscribetotheshow to help me on my continued – and possibly foolish – journey. My Professional Organization for Web3, AI and whatever comes next, Alpha Collective (think YPO meets the Illuminati) is still a work in progress. Please visit www.alphacollective.xyz.

But there is significant news to share.

I become an EOS (Entrepreneurial Operating System) implementer, delving into the realm of business and leadership team coaching, helping business owners get what they want from their business so they can live a better life. Please visit my microsite at www.eosworldwide.com/joseph-jaffe.

Life presents us with unexpected paths. Sometimes, what we believed to be true proves false, while unforeseen realities and new possibilities emerge.

LIFE AS A PROJECT

In many ways, I have come to embrace the idea that life is a project. The ultimate project.

It has a distinct start and end date, with specific objectives, goals, dreams, and aspirations.

Every aspect of our lives can be viewed as a project. It transcends mere jobs or careers; it encompasses our entire existence. This perspective was shaped by my obsession with English football, where head coaches and managers often refer to their jobs as projects. They understand that their tenure will likely be short-lived; whether due to success or failure, they are going to move on sooner, rather than later.

Adopting this mindset, I now recognize three core projects: my show, my community, and my role as a teacher, facilitator, and coach. Strike that: my four projects. I forgot this book. My bad.

Life has shifted, challenging my preconceptions, and affirming my commitment to helping others. Whether through mentoring, teaching, advising, facilitating, lecturing, or coaching, my purpose remains clear—to inspire, provoke, and encourage individuals to become the best versions of themselves.

EMBRACING CHANGE

Through introspection and self-discovery, I have found peace amidst the chaos. Even the untimely passing of my mother, which prevented her from witnessing the completion of this leg of my journey, has brought me solace.

I believe she would want me to find strength and continue pursuing my aspirations.

Mom, I want you to know that I'll be okay, and I'll carry your love and guidance in my heart forever.

THE GIFT

In 2023, I had the opportunity to complete a very special coaching program: Positive Intelligence developed by master coach, Shirzad Chamine. As part of the program, I learnt about my 10 Saboteurs, led by the Judge, whom I named, The Narcissist, as well as the 5

Sage powers. It was all part of a Neuroplasticity rollercoaster, where every so-called bad thing that happens TO you can be seen as a gift.

My gift was the discovery of my why: *I help people get unstuck, return to growth, and* **become forever changed**.

It only took 52 years, the death of both my parents, being hit by an express train, falling off a wall and crushing my shoulder and elbow, emigrating, being laid off, closing down a company, COVID, heart surgery, and finally – but certainly not last - the passing of my mother, to discover it.

Talk about foreplay!

THESE ARE THE THINGS

I realize now why I didn't finish the book. It wasn't time. I needed the passing of my mother to wrap everything up in a neat untidy bow. I needed things to get definitively worse in order see even more clearer and clearly:

These are the things that don't happen to you...they happen FOR you.

What are the things that have happened to you?

What are the things that are happening for you right now?

What will **you** do now?

What will you do next?

The world is waiting. I am waiting.

Let's do this!

CHAPTER 1
THE THING ABOUT GLOBAL PANDEMICS

THE THING ABOUT GLOBAL PANDEMICS IS THAT THEY ARE, you know, global.

I was thinking about events in history that have happened and impacted the entire world the exact same way.

What are they?

Plagues feature highly of course. And there's the World Cup, I suppose.

Besides COVID-19, I'm not sure anything has EVER happened to the entire world at the same time; at the same level; at the same intensity.

Actually, I can only think of one other. The flood. Yes, the biblical one. The one that involved that Noah dude - the one that pretty much wiped out the entire world except for a bunch of animals (I don't think the dinosaurs made it) and a small group of humans who lived to tell the tale. Other than "the flood," there's probably nothing that has affected the world quite like this.

Now I know what you're thinking: what about war?

Of course, war impacts and has impacted. As have economic times as well. Recessions and depressions - one in particular. World War One and World War Two may have had the word "world" inserted in their descriptions, but did they in fact affect the entire world at the same time, in the same way? No they did not. For starters, if you were on team Adolph, you experienced a very different war to that

CHAPTER 1 - THE THING ABOUT GLOBAL PANDEMICS

of Team "Rest of the World" and I'm fairly certain, the residents of the Galapagos were not as impacted as those of Poland.

We've **all** just lived through, and quite frankly might still be living through for the rest of our lives, including – but not limited to - all the PTSD that so many of us are facing, either getting sick ourselves, watching those we love going through hell – not to mention all the lives that were lost – a shared dystopian nightmare.

So how did we stack up?

DIVIDED WE STAND. DIVIDED WE FALL

There are only three things that can bring a country and even the world together. Just 3 things (trust me I've done the research) For the sake of this argument, I'll just focus on the US, led by the overly partisan dysfunctional government.

> Courtesy of Ronald Reagan
>
> *An evangelical minister and a politician arrived at Heaven's Gate one day together. St. Peter, after doing all the necessary formalities, took them in hand to show them where their quarters would be. And he took them to a small single room with a bed, a chair and a table and said, this was for the clergyman, and the politician was a little worried about what might be in store for him. And he couldn't believe it when St. Peter stopped in front of a beautiful mansion, with lovely grounds, many servants and told him that these would be his quarters. He couldn't help but ask - he said, "but wait, there's something wrong. How do I get this mansion while that good and holy man only gets a single room?" Then St. Peter says, "you have to understand how things are up here. We get thousands and thousands of clergy, but you're the first politician whoever made it.*

1. WAR, WAR IS STUPID.

To illustrate this point, I'll refer to the invasion of Iraq following 9/11. For a brief moment, the entire country was unified. With the exception of a handful of dissidents who used that moment to run for office on the I-told-you-so ticket, for the most part Democrats and Republicans were still reeling and hurting at what seemed like a movie plot come to life: two planes flying into the Twin Towers. I will never forget the moment President George W Bush stood on that heap of mangled metal, dirt, debris, and probably human remains addressing the nation and in truth, the world. And then one of the first responders shouted out, *"We can't hear you!"* And so W was handed a megaphone and replied, *"I can hear you! I can hear you! The rest of the world hears you. And the people who knocked these buildings down will hear all of us soon."*

Everyone cheered. The world cheered. I cheered. As chants of U.S.A. U.S.A. U.S.A. rang from the crowd, it was time to tap into the "Weapons of Mass Destruction" talking point from the weaponization of fear playbook that would later fiercely divide the country. As it turns out, there weren't any and so it appears war was *not* the great unifier.

2. A GLOBAL PANDEMIC.

Cue the main event. Certainly in this book.

One would think a global pandemic would absolutely bring the world, a country, a state, a city, a town...let's go even more hyperlocal...how about a neighborhood, a street, a house: a family together. You would be wrong. In this case, fierce debates arose. To mask, or not to mask? Is *that* the question? To vaccinate, or not to vaccinate? Surely that's not the question?!

And we're back to the weaponization playbook: this time, vaccination. Regardless of your views - I'll try and stay as impartial as Switzerland (minus the Nazi gold storage, of course) – we should have

CHAPTER 1 - THE THING ABOUT GLOBAL PANDEMICS

been as "thick as thieves" when it came to figuring out how to beat this virus.

I keep thinking back to what would have happened if everyone had just stayed indoors for two weeks. Could we have, in fact, hashtag stopped the spread?

We'll never know.

3. ALIEN INVASION

So if it isn't war (strike 1), and if it isn't a global pandemic (strike 2), we only have one strike left, and that is reserved for the (inevitable) alien invasion. As the government continues to declassify all the mystery that has been surrounding Area 51 and all those YouTube and TikTok videos, it appears we are **not** alone.

My prediction? Swing and a miss.

Good luck on that one. We're all going to need it.

When we **do** find out we're not alone and become the focus of either "War of the Worlds" or "Close Encounters," here's a safe prediction based on our first two whiffs at the plate...you guessed it, the weaponization playbook. Probably literally.

The social media and cable news network debates will be deafening: To friend or not to friend? We'll be labeled as anti-frienders or pro-invasion. The only similarity with "Independence Day" will be (another) slap in the face by Will Smith. First contact and any hope of joining The Federation will be quashed with squabbles and partisan debates.

Strike 3, but fear not as the aliens will either abandon their plans and give up on us #smh, or they'll die from laughter.

THE THING ABOUT GLOBAL PANDEMICS...

...is that they're global.

FOREVER CHANGED

Every person. On this earth. In every country. Faced with the same challenge; the same uncertainty; the same fears.

It was incredible to see people from Dubai to Durban. From Seoul to Sydney. From London to Lima. *Everyone* was in the same boat. And I will tell you that even going back to the conversation about war and recession and all the events that have affected the world throughout history, none could have affected the world quite like this. With Elon Musk's Town Square, nothing was isolated or insulated; everything was on the table. Let's call it the reverse-Rodriguez effect. R.I.P.

We were as connected and informed (allegedly) as the Borg and yet, to quote another Biblical doozy, we chose the Tower of Babel route. A fragmented, proliferated and garbled cacophony of forked tongues, defying the most obvious sign from a higher power running the *Schmatta District in the Sky*: to **shut the fuck up**. The sign? A simple piece of fabric...a mask.

But we can't go back in Search of Sugarman to blissfully ignorant, simply because of the world we live in today. A world of "perfect" information. A world of instant communication. A world of 24-hour cable news networks. A world filled with IM's and DM's and PM's. Pings and notifications. A world where everything is at our fingertips and yet everything seems to slip through our fingers. A world where we are more connected than ever before in history and yet, we are lonelier and more disconnected than ever before.

We were all on the same page as in Google.com. We were all experiencing this anomaly in real-time (even those hanging out in virtual worlds). Everyone in the same leaky boat at the same time. Conceptually operating on a level playing field. Where cooperation and collaboration could have been at the most intense, incredible level. But it didn't really happen. For-profit companies were in a race to come up with a vaccine first. Because there was money on the line.

CHAPTER 1 - THE THING ABOUT GLOBAL PANDEMICS

And China, the very country where this pandemic emanated from, was just being China. Oh, don't worry about them... it's just China being China. To this day, we're still not 100% sure whether this all came from a bat or a lab... or a bat in a lab... or a cat in the hat with a bat. In many respects, it's irrelevant.

The great pause was, in fact, a great reset. A great opportunity for EVERYONE, and I mean EVERYONE, to get back on the same page in the same playbook. To reconnect with those we had lost - both dead AND dead to you (through division.) To get back to a level playing field after so many people had lost their livelihoods and for others, their lives. Unless, of course, if you were The Clorox Company, waking up the day after all the shit hit the fan with a thriving money tree planted outside. Life was great. Life was grand. Clorox was hiring when everyone else was firing and laying off. They're probably firing now (see: AI) Must be nice when your product goes from a nice-to-have to a have-to-have overnight. Like the airport security business after 9/11. Poor airlines, they seem to suffer every single time. Perhaps it's just karma for all those delays, canceled flights, bad service, and airline food.

I digress.

WHERE WERE YOU?

Where were you when this all started?

I want you to put this book down **right now**. Or hit the pause button if you're listening to it on audio. I want you to stop and immediately do what I'm doing right now. Start recording or writing down your story.

Don't you forget, don't you *dare* forget, don't you dare!

Don't let these moments turn into faded memories. Don't let firsthand accounts and experiences become secondhand and thirdhand anecdotes that are exaggerated, diluted, or worse, forgotten.

FOREVER CHANGED

Go write it down right now.

I'll wait.

Where were you when the world shut down?

And when I say, where were you, I mean, <u>exactly</u> where were you to the square inch? What day, what time? What location? What were you doing? What sounds were you hearing? What smells were you smelling? What were you eating? What were you thinking? How did it affect you? How did it affect those that you loved? It's important to go back to this.

Your equivalent of Ground Zero or Day Zero.

It's vital to be able to represent your feelings as they were then. Raw emotions, hopes, dreams, fears. Put them in writing. Your account may be as compelling as mine. Probably more compelling than mine.

I'd like to hear your story, but first let me tell you my story.

And in many respects, my story is your story. And in others, it isn't. Your story is your story, and your story is as compelling, if not more compelling than my story is to you. Because it's your story.

And to the people that love you, your story is the only story that matters.

Now go and tell it.

CHAPTER 2
PRELUDE TO A PANDEMIC

To tell you my story, I'm going to share something with you I haven't really shared publicly. Or even privately. I'd been struggling before the pandemic. To set the stage, I probably have to go back to 2010 when I sold my company, crayon. I made some money, real money, and I built a house with it. It's the house that I live in today. I don't know whether I'll be living in the house in 20- or 10-years' time. Or even next year. It depends on how many people buy this book I guess. It was good while it lasted, but it's just a container. You can't eat bricks.

Don't get me wrong - I'm all for walls, floors, and a roof, but what it's made of - the materials, the fixtures, the fittings, the finishes - is less important. Nor where it's located. Beach or Boonies. Country, state, town. Just details. Cut, paste, mix or match.

All interchangeable and all replaceable. What is not replaceable however: Me. You. Nothing can replace me, and nothing can replace you.

Back to the story. I sold my company and shortly afterwards, I exited. I had a decision to make. I was at a fork in the road. Do I start a new company (which I did) or just focus on scaling my thought leadership business and, in doing so, become what I call a "chronic" public speaker? Looking back, it's not entirely clear I should have done the latter (hello COVID), because I would not be where I am right now. Good, Bad or Ugly.

I went with the former.

FOREVER CHANGED

I started a company to see if I could capture lightning in a bottle a second time round (spoiler alert: I could not). During this 5-year period, there were some good years and ok years and ultimately, some bad years for Evol8tion (pronounced Evolution.)

Turns out the vision of connecting startups and brands was not ready yet for Prime Time.

What if Kodak had started Instagram? What if Marriott had incubated Airbnb? What if Blockbuster had acquired Netflix?

To this day, I still believe in the vision of connecting Madison Avenue and Mountain View and in doing so, helping brands find their startup soulmates. Big laboring brands are, for the most part, flat. Plateauing. Even declining. The real growth is not coming from the legacy companies. Most of them are floundering these days.

If you want more proof of this, I'd recommend the book, "Built to Suck" by Joseph Jaffe (I can vouch for him), which was conveniently released in 2019.

There were many learnings from the final years at Evol8tion, but here are three I want to share with you today.

1. DON'T PROLONG THE AGONY.

Don't be afraid to pronounce time of death. If I had been decisive and chosen to close down and shutter Evol8tion two years earlier, who knows where I might have been today. I certainly would not have begun to drain my life savings, but I'll tell you one thing. I wouldn't be here. I wouldn't be writing this book. I wouldn't be forever changed.

You HAVE to believe that every single thing that has happened to you up until now has happened for a reason. It has molded you, shaped you, turned you, transformed you into who you are today or who you will be tomorrow. Your time may not have arrived yet, but

CHAPTER 2 - PRELUDE TO A PANDEMIC

it will. It can, it has to, it must, and only if you are paying attention and can stay the course.

So why didn't I act decisively two years' prior? Perhaps it was due to pride. Ego. Stubbornness. Greed. Fear. Fear of failure. Fear of being exposed as an imposter. We all have it. If you're not afraid, you're not alive. And so, I kept going until eventually the sun had set. It was dark. It was cold. I kept going because I believed then, as I believe today, in me. I chose me. Maybe that's another bad habit that just won't go away.

Or to quote legendary NFL coach Vince Lombardi, who took his Green Bay Packers to two Super Bowl wins: *"In all my days in all my life, I never lost a single game. I just ran out of time."*

I absolutely believe in what I call *"the holding pattern."* Circling in the air until you are called to land; until your number is called, until your time arrives.

The problem of course, is that persistence may be a mind superpower, but it still requires bodily fuel, and without it, we fatigue both mentally and physically. We run out of gas, and when we do, we crash and burn.

So, that was the first learning. When you see the signs, or as Yogi Berra would have said, *when you come to a fork in the road, take it.* The problem, however, is that often times you don't recognize you're at that proverbial fork in the road. And so you keep going, and while I would argue that your first goal is to recognize the signs for what they are and make the right choice, making the wrong choice as early as possible is still better long-term than being hamstrung and not making any choice... analysis paralysis. The road not taken.

2. TIMING IS EVERYTHING

Q. What's the key to a good jok....

FOREVER CHANGED

A. Timing!

(Works better out loud versus in text!)

My second learning during this period was about the importance of timing and luck. The Blue-Chip Brands were just not ready for this big vision. I still don't believe that they are. I'm not sure they ever will be. Too busy focusing on AI, automation, cost-cutting, and *chicken-little* activities. They should though. I don't know if they'll ever get there.

In many respects, we really are just playing the same record, and it's a broken record that plays over and over again and keeps getting stuck in the same place. If we've learned anything about history, it is that it keeps repeating itself over and over again and we just don't learn our lessons.

I've thought long and hard about why smart people make dumb decisions. Why educated and tenured people working for mighty corporations make dumb decisions? And specifically, why they don't learn from their dumb decisions and why they continue to make more dumb decisions. And then it hit me. It's not them making the same dumb decisions. They've moved on to make dumb decisions in new roles, departments, or countries within their company or at entire new companies. And the new intake of replacements are unwittingly, unknowingly making the same dumb decisions. You see, there's no continuity or consistency inside corporations. Whomever decided that job rotation was a good idea was one hell of a sadist. At least that's what I tell myself. It's not that they weren't ready for ME or MY visions. They just weren't ready. Period.

So kudos to the New York Times for purchasing Wordle. Perhaps I should change my show's name to Jaffdle. Quick moves. Quick pickups. Quick acquisitions. When you see a sign of life, when you see proof of life, snap it up.

CHAPTER 2 - PRELUDE TO A PANDEMIC

Our time on this earth is limited, both as human beings and the companies' said humans work for. When opportunity knocks, that's when we need to act decisively, comprehensively, and with conviction – FIRE. READY. AIM! And while that might not sound like a strategy, it is. It is an operational survival strategy.

So that was my second lesson. The timing wasn't right. I needed more time. I ran out of time. If I could do it all over again, perhaps I would have made it a little less lofty. Or dumbed it down. Startup acquisition for dummies.

And as for luck, I could give you my go-to Gary Player line, *"the more I practice, the luckier I get"* but instead, I'll go with Damon Centola, Professor at Penn, author of Change, who said on my show, *"luck is just the absence of science."*

Actually, I'll hit you with one of my other favorite quotes, *"luck is what happens when preparation meets opportunity"* and there's a twist here and it's a big one: if you think you're **unlucky**, it's actually just one of two things – or a combination of both: you need to prepare more and/or your opportunity just hasn't present itself...yet!

3. DISCIPLINE, ACCOUNTABILITY AND EXECUTION TRUMP VISION (DAMN, HATE TO ADMIT THAT)

I firmly believe had my business been running on EOS, I might be sipping a Pina Colada on a beautiful Caribbean beach right now. I did their organizational checkup retroactively for Evol8tion at its peak and scored a paltry 45 out of 100. EOS typically helps its clients get to around 80 within two years of implementing the system and tools. See how your business fares at:

http://bit.ly/TakeTheOrganizationalCheckUp

Case in point, I was the Visionary, interfering with the Integrator. We had the wrong people in the wrong seats (including me). We had no Scorecard. The vision was not shared by all. We had no meeting discipline. I could go on....

JOSEPH JAFFE: KEYNOTE SPEAKER V2.0 (BETA)

Evol8tion had hit its Ice Age. See what I just did there?

Time of Death. Time to move on and so I went back to basics. I went back to school. I even enrolled in a one-day program where I was paired up with bright-eyed and bushy-tailed speaker wannabes and a bunch of cranky OGs who were probably there for the same reason I was, reboot their speaking careers.

It was a useful program. There's no shame in showing up to class.

I'll never forget this one liner that really stuck with me: *"If you treat your speaking like a hobby, you'll be paid like it's a hobby, but if you treat it like a business, you'll be paid like it's a business."*

You see, when life was great for me as a speaker, I never imagined a time when it wouldn't be. Having spoken in 50+ countries and on every continent but Antarctica (call me!), my pipeline flowed vigorously, until it didn't. And suddenly, everyone was a keynote – or virtual - speaker (at least that's what their LinkedIn bio says, along with life coach, digital maven, social media ninja, web3 guru, and AI expert.)

I was – and still am - one of the best in the business (my speaker reel is on www.josephjaffe.com), but no one knew it anymore. Or cared. I was the tree falling in the forest, and it doesn't matter if I made a whimper or not because **you weren't there**.

So I put together a new rate card. And a one pager. I started reaching out to speaker bureaus and I even launched my first speaker website. I didn't even have a funnel, traditional or flipped! I went back to the basics and followed all the steps I had seemingly skipped when life was grand.

CHAPTER 2 - PRELUDE TO A PANDEMIC

And that's the thing, of course. When life is great, THAT'S when you should be working even harder and hustling even harder because there's going to come a time when things aren't so great, and that's when you're going to find out one way or the other, often the hard way, whether all that preparation, planning, and hard work is going to give you the wiggle room - the breathing space to live to fight another day.

> Excerpt from my interview with Ross Bernstein on my show:
>
> *Great coaches in sports know how to manage emotions, so you don't get too high with success or too low with failure. It's about finding a balance. Herb Brooks is one of my favorite examples – he was the coach of the 1980 US Olympic 'Miracle on Ice' hockey team.*
>
> *Most people when we're not hitting our numbers in the sales team, we fire people yell at them, we punish them. And when things are going well, we say if it ain't broke, don't fix it. Herb was the opposite. He was a reverse psychologist, so when his teams were playing well, and they were dominating, he put the hammer down and he asked for more. He would punish them. He'd make him skate, he'd make them work because he knew that they had more to give.*
>
> *And then conversely, when they were playing poorly, and they were in a slump, he'd back off the gas. he'd send them out, get them their own team bus, cancel a plane ride home and tap a keg, buy a bunch of pizzas and let them just let their hair down. And invariably, it would work itself out and they would come back and they would recover much quicker from that slump.*

Of course, this is not to say you shouldn't work hard when times are tough. It's just that there's no business during the down days. And if I've learned anything, it's that when people don't want to buy, they're not going to buy.

FOREVER CHANGED

When things are good, you need to be at your paranoid and vigilant peak, wondering if you've hit the top and whether the freefall is about to set in.

And so I went back to basics.

And I went back to school.

New book released in 2019.

I was ready to hit the speaking circuit.

I was ready to hit the road.

March 2020.

And you know what happened next...

CHAPTER 3
PRIORITIES

LET ME TELL YOU MY STORY, AND MY STORY IS YOUR STORY. AND I'm not special. I'm not better than you or worse than you; I'm different and the same. This is my story, if you'll hear it. You have a story too, and your story is as compelling, relevant, interesting, and as important as mine. In fact, your story is the most important story of all.

I want you to tell your story. Write it down. Make sure it's passed down from generation to generation. Because at the end of the day, your kids, grandkids, and great grandkids shouldn't have to care about some arbitrary person's story like mine. They should know about your moments of truth, the points in the road, the decisions taken and not taken—the triumphs, the tragedies, and the regrets that made you better, stronger, tougher, and more resilient than anyone could have ever imagined.

HINDSIGHT IS 20/20

If hindsight is 20/20, I'd rather be blind. 2020 sucked. Royally. The Global Pandemic may be the focus and backdrop of this book, but let's be clear: alongside the injury of COVID-19, we need to add the insult of political turmoil, racial injustice, the rise of nationalism, isolationism, xenophobia, war, **and** the loss of Kobe. One of the most ridiculous things that happened during the Global Pandemic had nothing to do with the virus itself – at least not directly. We allowed partisan bullshit, political talking points and self-serving talking heads to tear relationships and families apart.

When people refer to this period as a Great Pause or Reset, perhaps we should do just that. We need to pause and reset; go back, repair and mend all these fences we've torn down. This pandemic should have woken us up from our slumber, given us a kick in the you-know-where to get our priorities straight. Family. Friendship. Health. Happiness.

Priorities.

I think back to the hundreds or thousands of hours people spent "debating" but really just screaming at – and talking over - each other on Clubhouse, Talk Radio, Fox News, Twitter and any other town square that welcomed and monetized despair. What was the point? All that energy. All that potential. Wasted!

ROAD WARRIORS OR WORRIERS?

Priorities.

Take travel, for example. To those who took pride on living out of a suitcase, were you moving towards your calling or true purpose (Traction), or knowingly running away from—or unconsciously avoiding—an inconvenient truth (Distraction)? I get it, work is work, jobs to be done. Sometimes we don't get to decide when we need to attend a meeting, event, or conference. But with that said, we didn't really put up a fuss, did we? We submitted to the trimmings and trappings of business travel a little too easily.

Miss those warm (that often times weren't warm at all) nuts in Business Class on American Airlines? Boy, do I have the greatest life hack for you. It's called Planters and a Microwave. You're welcome.

Fortunately, travel has become such a nightmare these days that our decisions are being made for us. There's a reason why we've been warned against B.Y.O.A. (Bring Your Own Alcohol). People are going postal on planes, because they are either broken or at their breaking points.

CHAPTER 3 - PRIORITIES

I used to count down the minutes to those forgettable moments on American Airlines when I sipped my cheap, warm Prosecco from a plastic faux champagne flute or lay my head down on a "flat bed" which was as hard as nails and probably still warm from the last lard ass who farted the night away the evening before. Sorry to be so graphic, but it is what it is.

RETHINKING TRAVEL: PRIORITIZING LIFE

These days, if you want to book me for a speaking engagement (which I barely do anymore), you'll get the best pricing on virtual keynotes and the worst on international and in-person keynotes. The reason is simple, and the signal I'm sending out is clear: *I don't want to travel. I don't need to travel. WE don't need to travel.*

People who covet George Clooney's character in "Up in the Air" are as lost as Ryan Bingham was. You shouldn't have to look forward to a flight with a lie-flat bed when you already have a lie-flat bed at home minus the noise of the plane, the circulating sick air, the awful plane food, or a $9.99 "French" Bordeaux.

Don't get me wrong (why do people say that?) I'm not knocking the importance of in-person networking or even the serendipity of talking to strangers. Thank you, Malcolm Gladwell! It's a powerful concept, but we can do that right now on platforms like Discord or Zoom. We can develop real relationships in virtual worlds without ever meeting in person. The concept is called *asynchronous intimacy*. We can experience what I call *socialdipity* —serendipity in a social era or perhaps we call it *metadipity*—serendipity in the metaverse.

We can still benefit from human interaction without leaving our homes. I enjoy face-to-face interactions as much as the next person. I appreciate the game of networking, where conference attendees stare at each other's midriffs to catch a quick glance at their name tags, titles and company names to determine if they are important enough to make small talk with. I cherish hearing strangers complaining about their office politics from their overpaid jobs.

I can do it all in a breakout room on Zoom and I don't even have to wear pants in the process.

CHANGE THAT CHANNEL

Years ago, I was flying back to the US after giving a keynote in Europe. Sipping on my screw top $9.95 red wine, I watched a movie called "Click." It stars Adam Sandler and the legendary Christopher Walken, who plays an angel that gives Adam Sandler's character a magical remote control. Among other things, the remote control allows him to pause, play, and fast forward moments in his life, including arguments with his wife (woohoo!) A simple fast forward lets him skip through disagreements. Even better, the remote control *learns* his viewing habits and preferences, skipping interruptions and domestic squabbles.

And then one day, he wakes up, and his entire life has been fast-forwarded. He sees strangers he doesn't recognize, only to realize they're his grown-up kids now holding his grandchildren. He realizes that he's missed their childhood because he fast-forwarded through it—through his own life. That scene hit me hard, and I couldn't hold back my tears. I was almost inconsolable, with flight attendants approaching me, concerned and offering assistance. It was a moment reminiscent of the movie "Airplane," with my emotional state resembling hysteria. People were lining up with baseball bats, guns and crowbars.

Adam was me. George was me. I was missing out on the precious moments of my own life.

The Great Joe Jaffe, star of the show, keynoter, headliner, Executive Platinum, 50+ countries (Peru is still on my bucket list), staying in fancy hotels, visiting exotic countries, flying first class. Yet, I was

CHAPTER 3 - PRIORITIES

missing in action, absent from the first steps, the first words, the highs and lows. I found out about these magical moments through impersonal text messages and emails—someone else's memory of my own family. And in that moment, I sobbed.

This was our life before the pandemic, at least for those of us deemed "successful." The C-suite life, which perhaps should be called the C-Sour. To climb the corporate ladder, it was expected to be constantly up in the air, traveling daily and weekly. And it wasn't just about living in different cities within a single country but across continents—China, Germany, Brazil. Our poor kids and spouse were constantly playing catch-up, holding on, putting on a brave face to show support as they settled in at the International School.

We forced them to adapt to new environments, make new friends, navigate language barriers, face the pressures of social media. Who's the weird new kid?

Was all of this really necessary?

I understand the rationale behind it—to succeed in a corporation, you need versatility, understanding different cultures; experience in various departments, geographies, business units, and P&Ls. But just because something is common practice doesn't mean it's right or fair. That was the price we paid—the sacrifice our families made for companies that were Built to Suck.

And here's the irony—today, job security within corporations is far from secure. The Talent War may be the number one priority for corporations—how to attract, retain, activate, and maximize it, but they're losing it big time. The Great Resignation works both ways. Employers have resigned themselves to losing their best and brightest because they've given up on investing in training and development. They recognize that talent is temporary, and employees no longer view companies as lifelong appointments. Loyalty is scarce. Loyalty is fleeting.

FOREVER CHANGED

Companies discard their talent like scraps as they drool over all those cost savings from AI bots.

Who could ever forget Better.com CEO Vishal Garg, who announced the mortgage company was laying off about 9% of its workforce on a Zoom webinar, abruptly informing the more than 900 employees on the call they were being terminated *just before the holidays*.

"If you're on this call, you are part of the unlucky group that is being laid off...Your employment here is terminated effective immediately." Wait it gets better, *"This is the second time in my career I'm doing this...the last time I did it, I cried."*

Or how about Andi Owen, CEO of MillerKnoll. She received a bonus of nearly $4,000,000 in 2022 and then told her employees via video when addressing their concerns about income shortfall, *"Don't ask about 'what are we going to do if we don't get a bonus?' Get the damn $26 million."* She added insult to injury with, *"I had an old boss who said to me one time, 'You can visit Pity City, but you can't live there.' So, people, leave Pity City. Let's get it done."*

Congratulations Vishal and Andi, you are now both immortalized in the Hall of Shame.

The only retirement party these days is for the company itself, struggling to stay afloat amidst constant disruption. The pandemic, as many predicted, acted as a great accelerator, hastening the demise of many businesses. Here today, gone tomorrow—this is the essence of the broken business model of big business. Size, scale, and economies of scale have become burdens, slowing them down in a world that's speeding up.

As Chris Fuller said to me on "Joseph Jaffe is not Famous, *"...at scale, cracks become chasms."*

CHAPTER 3 - PRIORITIES

The safety net of the corporate world is riddled with gaping holes

The safety net of the corporate world is riddled with gaping holes. I don't want my children to go through this. I want to encourage them to be in charge of their own lives, masters of their own destiny.

WEB3 MAY HOLD THE KEY

Corporations should start looking at employees the way we look at NFT (non-fungible tokens) collections. As the founder of a collection, your goal is to create a community where every member cherishes their NFT (soulbound) and would never want to sell it for any amount of money. Similarly, as an HR professional, your aim should be to create an environment where employees never want to leave.

How can this be achieved? By treating employees exceptionally well, fostering a culture that values both monetary and non-monetary benefits (they call this "utility"), having a clear company purpose and point of view, and taking a stand on important issues. For example, a company that pays for women to have abortions and covers any legal fees when crossing state lines because it believes it's the right thing to do. This is the kind of community and company where I want to belong—and why shouldn't those terms be interchangeable?

I remember when I started working at Ogilvy in 1997, earning $40,000. Coming from South Africa, I couldn't believe the amount of money I was making. But then, DMB&B offered me $65,000 and I was tempted to leave. In a last-ditch effort to keep me, my boss' boss' boss' boss called me into his office. He said he didn't want me to go (wait, you know my name?), and I didn't want to go either.

What would it take to keep you, Joe?

So I asked him to match the offer. But he couldn't, not because he didn't want to, but because it came from the retention budget, which had a cap.

He offered me a raise of $10,000.

I left.

They lost me for $15,000— an amount that felt significant then (at least for me), but now was clearly insignificant. It turned out to be the worst decision for <u>both</u> parties. Imagine where I would be today if I had stayed. Imagine where Ogilvy would be. With that said, in all likelihood, I would have probably been laid off.

PRIORITIZATION ABOVE MONEY

Looking back now, with more wisdom and a few more gray hairs, I wonder: What if I had gone back to them and said, *"I'll stay because it's not about the money."* Why does loyalty have to be one-sided?

Nah, I probably would have been laid off anyway.

Unless working there wasn't just a job, but perhaps part of an experience. With intangibles that were hard to quantify in monetary terms.

My vision is to have thousands of people in the virtual Collective Cafe coffee shop every weekday morning. What better way to start off your day than with manifesting, motivation, thought leadership, insights, leadership and skills advice and so much more. I run a virtual coffee shop every Monday - Friday from 8-9am EST.

I believe every company will have their own version of a virtual coffee every workday morning

An audio-first and audio-only experience as people are commuting, hitting the treadmill, walking the dog, or getting the kids ready for school.

CHAPTER 3 - PRIORITIES

What better way to transform a company into a community, and a community into an experience? Community may be the last hope for the corporation. And it begins with a Cup of Joe. Well not me, but I'm happy to join you one day if you like.

Until companies can figure out how to solve for the horribly broken commute, health care, childcare, and some kind of antidote or cure for the Cube Farm blues – and no, a medical procedure like in the series Severance is NOT on the table – we are not going to see companies growing like they need to. If they do not regard their people as priorities, how on earth do they think their people will make them a priority in return?

I'm not going to hold my breath that companies are going to embrace this any time soon, but at the same time, your employees aren't going to be holding their breath either.

Whether you are a road warrior or worrier, a boss, or an employee, what are your priorities? What matters? What counts? At the end of the day, when you put your head on the pillow, are you 30,000 feet in the air or grounded with what truly matters?

Thank you Pandemic for opening our eyes.

Finally.

CHAPTER 4
OH YEAH, I NEED OPEN HEART SURGERY

I TURNED 50 ON DECEMBER 24, 2020. YET ANOTHER THING THAT sucked in 2020, but to be honest with you, I was actually okay turning the big 5-0.

No celebrations involving travel or big parties took place due to the pandemic. Instead, something rather unique and special: my wife organized a *surprise drive-by celebration* at Compo Beach in Westport.

Under the guise of going for a walk along the beach, we arrived and saw our family and friends, socially distanced and wearing masks, holding signs and balloons. I went down the line, high-fiving people and spending time with each group. It was a special and surreal experience.

FACING THE REALITY OF TURNING 50

One of the things that comes with turning 50 is going for a physical. Let me take this opportunity for a public service announcement: men - get your prostate checked, everyone - get your annual physical. It's essential and a no-brainer and in my case, it most definitively saved my life...

Another PSA (fast forward to 2022), I had my first colonoscopy. The supervising doctor even complimented me on having one of the cleanest colons he had ever seen. Perhaps too much information, but there you go. At this age, you take (and share) any compliments you can get.

I went for my physical towards the end of March 2021. Appointments weren't that easy to come by because of COVID, but I was

CHAPTER 4 - OH YEAH, I NEED OPEN HEART SURGERY

also dragging my feet because I didn't see the urgency. I was at the top of my physical game. I was in great shape, thanks to regular running on the road and cycling on my Peloton.

During the physical, everything seemed to be going well. My vitals checked out and my prostate was clear. My primary care physician concluded that everything seemed great, except for one thing: the murmur....

PROBABLY NOTHING

"Everything's great except for – you know - the murmur," he said casually. I was taken aback. *"Mur-what?"* I asked, puzzled.

To be "safe", he recommended I go for an echocardiogram. I didn't think much of it at the time.

I mentioned it to my family, and my sister said she had a murmur too. Research shows that around 20-25% of people have some kind of murmur, often caused by a prolapse of the mitral valve. It's a normal occurrence and nothing to worry about.

I took my time and went for the echocardiogram on a Monday towards the end of April. Prior to the test, I had crushed two back-to-back one-hour Endurance Power Zone sessions on my Peloton over the weekend. #teamwilpers. I was feeling strong and fit.

UNEXPECTED NEWS: OPEN HEART SURGERY

The week unfolded like this:

Monday morning, April 26: Echocardiogram.

Monday afternoon, April 26: Call from the cardiologist to discuss the results. He suggests coming in the next day. Scheduling Gods were smiling or so I thought...

Tuesday afternoon, April 27: The cardiologist informs me that I *definitely* need open heart surgery.

FOREVER CHANGED

Wednesday, April 28: Appointment booked with my soon-to-be heart surgeon.

I was in complete disbelief. I was healthy, fit, and only 50 years young. I asked the doctor if a second opinion would make sense. He replied that I could get one, but it would 100% confirm the need for open heart surgery to repair my "mitral valve prolapse with severe regurgitation." Technically, my chordae had ruptured. Or to use an analogy: several strings on a parachute or the cords on a blind or curtain had snapped and were not fully functioning.

I remember driving home on the I-95 South, calling my wife and dropping the bombshell. Now it was her turn to be shocked and express disbelief.

On May 17, I met with the heart surgeon who confirmed what I already knew. We scheduled the procedure for June 22. I also had to choose between a cow, pig, or mechanical valve as a backup option in case the repair became a replacement. An animal valve was "set it and forget it" but would require another surgery in about 10 years, whereas the mechanical valve came with a "lifetime guarantee," but I would need to take a blood thinner every day for the rest of my life. For a young man like myself, the Bull (as in Mechanical) option seemed more than palatable considering the circumstances.

I was also advised to avoid getting my heart rate above 120 beats per minute, which meant I had to stop exercising. For someone like me, who believes in the strong connection between a healthy body and a healthy mind, this restriction was mentally taxing. The inability to exercise and release those endorphins was sure to have an impact on my mental health.

It did.

When I can't exercise, I tend to put on weight. When I put on weight, I get depressed.

CHAPTER 4 - OH YEAH, I NEED OPEN HEART SURGERY

SHARING MY JOURNEY

Despite the difficult news, I made a decision not to hide or retreat into my shell. I had a talk show and a public persona, and I believed it was important to be open and transparent with my community. I didn't believe in selectively choosing what to share, nor trauma dumping,

I shared exactly what was happening, creating a countdown to the surgery and even created a GoFundMe-like campaign. People could support me, and in return, I would provide them with benefits, perks, and experiences associated with my talk show. It felt like a genuine and meaningful way to engage with my community.

THE DAY OF SURGERY

The days leading up to June 22 were some of the most difficult of my life. I had to give up caffeine and alcohol - saying goodbye to my beloved daily cups of coffee and COVID-inspired glasses of red wine. Decaffeinated coffee is NEVER OK!

The nerves were palpable, although maybe that was the lack of caffeine talking.

I don't remember much about the night before the surgery. I think there were dietary restrictions, but it felt like my last meal on Death Row, minus the spicy or fried foods.

As I finally fell asleep, the alarm went off. One of my children was vaping #FML

The surgery took place in Hartford, Connecticut, about 65 miles from my home.

I arrived with my wife, and it was beyond emotional. Tears flowed freely as we said our goodbyes. Due to COVID protocols, she couldn't accompany me inside. I was on my own as I entered the hospital.

FOREVER CHANGED

I had no idea what to expect. I underwent a COVID test, which felt like they were digging into my brain with that swab. I changed into a hospital gown that seemed like a sadist's dream to expose my backside. *I can feel it coming in the air tonight, O Lord.*

Then came the unexpected surprise: a thorough shave. My chest, legs, arms, and groin were all shaved in preparation for the surgery. It was a lesson in leaving shame at the door, as I quickly learned in the hospital.

As time passed, various drips and lines were inserted into my arms.

And then the phone rang. Not April Fool's but it might as well have been. It was the surgeon's scheduler calling to inform me that the surgery had been **canceled**. My surgeon had been called into an emergency surgery with complications, leaving him too exhausted to proceed as planned.

"How about July 14th?" the scheduler suggested.

I was furious. How could they just cancel open heart surgery? *"This isn't a fucking flight,"* I screamed in shock and anger. After waiting for more clarity for over an hour, I had had enough. I changed back into my clothes, called an Uber, and headed home, still wearing the hospital bracelet.

15 minutes into the ride, the scheduler called again. They asked if I could come back to Hartford the next morning at 5:30 am. I agreed, although I had been looking forward to a moment of respite and a double fisted mean glass of scotch and Venti coffee.

The next morning. I returned to the hospital, minus the shave, COVID test, and cancellation drama. The surgery was back on like Donkey Kong!

CHAPTER 4 - OH YEAH, I NEED OPEN HEART SURGERY

I met with the anesthesiologist, went through the necessary paperwork and waivers, including the minor risks involved in the procedure—heart attacks, stroke, even death. I signed the paperwork.

They wheeled me into the operating room, resembling a scene from a medical drama. Bright lights, numerous monitors, and an array of surgical instruments lined up. I rolled onto the bed, and as the surgical team began to introduce themselves one by on……….., I realized I had been tricked. The world faded into Bolivian (to quote Mike Tyson).

When I woke up, I found myself in the ICU with a breathing tube down my throat and a chest tube in my midriff. The pain was excruciating, and the sensation of drowning from the breathing tube was overwhelming. It felt like being waterboarded for what seemed like an eternity until they finally removed it a couple of hours later.

Despite the extreme discomfort, I had achieved my goals coming out of the procedure:

1. Don't Die
2. Successful Repair
3. Avoid the pig, cow or bull valves (in other words, no replacement)

The road to recovery was far from over.

The night in the ICU was filled with pain and medication. Every two hours, the nurses administered pain medication through an IV, and I drifted off to sleep, until I woke up in pain again. Rinse and Repeat.

The following day, I was moved to a step-down ward, and to my surprise, I was discharged from the hospital the very next day. It was hard to believe that I had gone in on a Wednesday and was heading home on a Friday. The reality of it seemed unreal, and little did I know that the dream would soon become a nightmare.

COMPLICATIONS AND SETBACKS

Returning home was both a relief and a new challenge. I was weak, but the feeling of being back in familiar surroundings was comforting. However, over the next few days, I developed a *seroma*—an accumulation of fluid in my upper leg and groin area due to severed lymphatic nodes during the surgery. It was the size of a softball. I grew increasingly worried.

I learned that in less than 5% of cases, a seroma develops after this type of surgery, and in less than 5% of those cases, it becomes infected. 0.25% against and 99.75% in favor of resolution.

Luck was not on my side. The seroma became infected.

One early Sunday morning, I found myself shivering with chills and running a high fever. We rushed back to the hospital in Hartford, where I spent the next 10 days back in the step-down ward. I was like Norm from Cheers as the nurses all greeted me. *"What are you doing back here so soon?"* they playfully bantered to lighten the mood. *"The usual?"*

I ended up with a second surgery and this one required a Wound-Vac machine (Google it) and Visiting Nurses at-home visits to allow the wound to heal from the inside out.

A couple of months later I developed cellulitis (skin infection) and was back in the hospital.

And then I got COVID, lost my sense of smell and taste, had monoclonal antibodies, but fortunately no bleach.

Hang on...not done yet. Less than 24 hours after I tested negative for COVID, I developed cellulitis again.

The fourth hospital stay was not uneventful after a SOP COVID test came back with a false positive. I became an instant pariah. Marked as a contagious patient. Warning signs were placed on my door, and

CHAPTER 4 - OH YEAH, I NEED OPEN HEART SURGERY

medical staff entered my room fully dressed in personal protective equipment.

The mind can play tricks on you in such situations. None of these complications should have happened. Wasn't open heart surgery enough for one person to endure? Instead of being deep into my rehabilitation and working my way up the Peloton leaderboards, I found myself studying hospital menus.

I have to admit, Bridgeport Hospital makes a mean Beyond Burger.

I had expected all of these challenges to be behind me before Labor Day, the first Monday in September. And yet, there I was in mid-December in Cardiac Rehab, being constantly scolded by Ms. Hannigan every time my heart rate monitor indicated that I was pushing too hard.

I was the youngest person in the rehab group by at least 20 years. This was NOT how I envisioned my recovery.

FINDING MOMENTUM

My Mitral Valve Prolapse made it incredibly challenging to establish any momentum. Every time I tried to get back on track, something would force me to pause or stop completely. It felt like playing a game of Snakes and Ladders, consistently landing on the longest snake and sliding all the way back to the beginning.

As I reflect on this journey, I realize that each "Déjà vu loop;" each setback was not an exact repetition of what came before. It wasn't Goundhog Day, but rather Independence Day – an opportunity to build resilience, stamina, determination, and endurance. What didn't kill me (literally) made me stronger.

Today, I'm immensely grateful for the ability to hop on a bike or go for a run, regardless of how short or how slow it may be. It's a gift to feel alive and be free.

FOREVER CHANGED

I'm simply grateful to be here in this very moment.

That, my friends, was 2021—a year that truly sucked way more than 2020. As we approached the end of that challenging year, I found myself rewriting the lyrics to a well-known holiday song:

"On the fourth day of Christmas, a cruel higher power gave to me... Four hospital stays, Three infections, Two surgeries, and a bout of COVID just for me!"

And scene.

CHAPTER 5
DO YOU WANT IT NOW?

It was 1994 and my mom and I found ourselves strolling through the streets of London. Fresh from a trip to the US, where we had the incredible opportunity to travel on the legendary Concorde—a privilege few can claim. London's ambiance surrounded us as we soaked in the impeccable English taste in fashion, clothing and style. I couldn't help but marvel at the amazing things I saw in the shop windows.

I saw a magnificent tie.

"Let me buy it for you Joseph."

"Oh no, it's way too expensive in South African Rands."

I saw an incredible suit.

"Let me buy it for you Joseph."

"I could never. It make me sick to my stomach how much that costs."

I gazed at a wonderful dress shirt.

"Let me buy it for you Joseph."

"Not a chance...not at that price!"

Each time, my mom offered to buy them for me, and each time I hesitated, dismissing them as too expensive as a I calculated the Rand/Pound exchange rate which I believe was 20:1 at the time. I just could not get over the price premium.

This back-and-forth continued until my mom reached a breaking point. With exasperation, she dropped her shopping bags (more like threw them to the ground) and asked me this profound question that would stay with me forever, "Do you want it now when I'm gone?"

"Do you want it now when I'm gone?"

That moment holds tremendous significance for me, especially now that my mom is gone, after battling cancer in South Africa for just shy of 7 years. It makes me question my priorities. It makes me question everything. What kind of quality of life is it when one foot is always in the grave, "planning for a rainy day" and – I get it – being **responsible**! Or can we find greater joy in being fully present with our loved ones and in doing so, soak up every iota of joy that comes from living in the moment and turning every opportunity into an experience?

COROLLARY

The scenario where those purchases could be made without the blink of an eye; dialed-in as it were. That's not the answer either. Clearly. Appreciating the moment is the real prize. Even if that moment ends up being emptied handed – **as long as it has a story, a glory, a context and a memory, it represents a life well lived.** A life filled with meaningful connections, presence, and purpose, but moreover a life that cherishes **shared experiences**, rather than a series of disconnected and isolated transactions.

EMBRACING OUR SIGNIFICANCE

Zooming out to contemplate our place in the vastness of existence, we have two choices. We can either view ourselves as insignificant grains of sand on a vast shore; specks of dust on the Earth; harmless (hopefully) bugs to the sentient AI machine. Or we can adopt an existential perspective, recognizing that the world was created

CHAPTER 5 - DO YOU WANT IT NOW?

for each of us. It's not about an egocentric or arrogant position but rather acknowledging the beauty of our individual existence. When we go to sleep, the world slumbers with us. Perhaps the entire world dies. Perhaps we die and return the next day to have another "at bat."

The world was built for us, and everyone around us plays a role in our unique narrative—even you, the reader, as you engage with this book. You are all part of my narrative and I appreciate you more than you will ever know.

We are walking miracles. The odds of us existing are miraculous.

If we assume 250 million sperm per ejaculation, and let's say one woman has about 400 viable eggs in her lifetime. If we consider only the last 10 generations of your ancestors (a very conservative estimate given that humans have been around for about 200,000 years), the odds of you being exactly as you are, come out to roughly 1 in $(250 \text{ million} \times 400)^{10}$. This number is so big that it's practically incalculable.

Now if you wanted to factor in the odds of any given individual existing in the first place, you'd have to consider the probability of life on Earth developing, human evolution occurring as it has, and the incredibly specific chain of reproduction leading to you. British cosmologist Sir Martin Rees has famously posited that the odds of the universe and life forming as we know it could be as low as 1 in a billion. Woohoo!

Or you could take a more philosophical perspective (Tom Morris, I see you!), and argue that the odds are, in fact, 100%. If you're able to ask the question, then you are alive, so the odds are a perfect 1:1.

I prefer to quote the great philosopher, Dr Seuss, who remarked, "Today you are You, that is truer than true. There is no one alive who is Youer than You."

If this is true, why would we choose to be passive spectators in our own lives? It's a rhetorical question, urging us to seize the moment and make the most of it.

RETHINKING LIFE INSURANCE

Life insurance or life assurance? The insurance industry, with its focus on health and life coverage, stands as one of the largest in the world. It offers products designed to care for us in times of illness or after our passing. But it's a curious product, as we pay monthly premiums with the hope that we never have to use them.

Let's consider a tale of a pig and a chicken walking down a road. The chicken suggests opening a restaurant called "ham-n-eggs," but the pig declines, noting that for the chicken, it's merely a side hustle, while for the pig, it's going all-in.

This analogy mirrors the distinction between life assurance, represented by the chicken, and life insurance, represented by the pig. Both cases revolve around the one thing money can't truly buy: health. It's a realization that further affirms the paradigm shift brought about by the events of #foreverchanged. We can count our money, but we can't count the remaining days we have on this Earth—or on Mars if Elon Musk's ambitions become reality. And by the time we can truly appreciate the value of time, it's often too late.

BREAKING FREE FROM THE SAFETY NET

We shouldn't be confined to living our lives in constant anticipation, preparation, and planning for our eventual death. Some people even accelerate this eventuality and take their lives into their own hands. It should never come to that. The impact of mental health on our lives compounded by personal, professional, and financial hardships that seem insurmountable—holes that seem too deep to climb out of – exacerbated by factors of our own doing – or undoing – like social media and presented with a giant COVID cherry on top!

CHAPTER 5 - DO YOU WANT IT NOW?

Loneliness is an epidemic and has been compared – in terms of its impact on longevity – to smoking half a pack of cigarettes a day.

It's worth noting that life insurance builds in suicide clauses or provisions. Failure in life. Failure in Death. It's not right.

You are not alone.

I recently wrote an eBook that offered 10 solutions to "when digging oneself in a hole." The first of course is to stop digging. You can download this ebook at foreverchanged.life

REDISCOVERING THE VALUE OF LIFE

Here's a thought: what about payouts when we're alive versus when we expire? Many of us are actually "existing" on the surface – waiting for the policy to "mature" - but on the inside, are already dead - devoid of life and passion. Instead of contemplating the roads we took versus the roads not taken – the safe route with the safety net, why not live a little? We build a life with so many guardrails, protections and guarantees, with life insurance, retirement plans, or simply a stable paycheck, that life becomes sanitized, predictable and vanilla. Why do we hold back?

"The thing about vanilla. It's the most popular flavor, but no one will travel across town for it." – Jeremy Tucker, ex-CMO of Planet Fitness on Joseph Jaffe is not Famous

EMBRACING THE JOURNEY OF LIFE

Every now and then you need a gutter ball or two.

We try and teach our children about the power of adversity and how things will always work out in the end. In the moment, they are blind to perspective. To them, the challenges they face—such as being deferred from their college of choice, cut from a sports team, or overlooked in an Instagram photo—feel like catastrophes of the highest order. Life, as they know it, ceases to exist. But as parents, we are able to step in and save the day. We become their guiding lights, their beacons of wisdom.

And besides, they always get a participation trophy!

As they end up going to the second college on their shortlist (or eventually getting into the first), excelling at a different sport or pursuing another passion, or finding a new tribe and circle of friends, they utter those inevitable and immortal words, *"you were right, Dad or Mom."* How was it that our parents were so smart; so wise; so informed; so calm?

Answer: they weren't.

As we grow older and become parents ourselves, we realize the truth—they were just making it up as they went along. As are we. We are just as clueless as they were. It's a lot like the life of an entrepreneur, always navigating uncharted territory. In fact, it's the essence of life itself. There is no definitive playbook, foolproof guidelines or sure things. Those who promise certainty will ultimately disappoint. Despite the uncertainty, we all find a way to land on our feet and make it through the challenges that come our way.

If I had known then what I know now, I would most likely not have gotten involved!

Bullshit. If I had known then what I know now, I would have gotten involved one year earlier!

> If I had known then what I know now, I would have gotten involved one year earlier!

CHAPTER 5 - DO YOU WANT IT NOW?

TAKING THE FIRST STEP

While there may not be a definitive playbook, there are signs along the way if we pay attention. We don't necessarily need to sever the safety net, but we must find the strength, confidence, conviction, and courage to take the first step toward living fully. Do we truly want to wait until it's too late? When we're gone, what remains? David Brooks talks about Resume Virtues versus Eulogy Virtues.

I've yet to attend a eulogy that prioritizes EBITDA over Empathy; Cost Savings over Kindness. Press Releases over Intimate Memories.

It's not about money, titles, or possessions. It's about time. Money may prolong our health and extend our time on this Earth, but it can't turn back time. Sorry, Cher.

JUST 5 MORE MINUTES

As I reflect on the times when I would visit my mom during her illness in South Africa, I recall moments when we would travel to the airport together. Approaching the terminal and the drop-off zone, I would find myself yearning for just five more minutes. Just five more minutes to spend with her. The value I would place on those precious moments was immeasurable. I would pay the world; I would give the world for that opportunity.

What I would have given for 5 more minutes to say that final goodbye versus that 3am call to find out she was unresponsive and 20 minutes later a second one to let me know she had passed.

Consider your own life. How much time have you wasted? How many moments have you taken for granted? How often have you been physically present but emotionally absent, buried in the distractions of technology? We've all been guilty of snapping a covert family photo where everyone is at the table, but on their phones. It's become a common occurrence in my household —a term we "playfully" coined "Iwasjus."

"Iwasjus checking the train schedule"

"Iwasjus looking at the weather."

"Iwasjus texting to see what time everyone was meeting later."

"Iwasjus reading an important email" (although in reality, Iwasjus checking my crypto portfolio)

Feel free to use the hashtag #iwasjus in your subversive social media shenanigans. Your unsuspecting victims may not know what you're up to, but I will. Who knows, maybe it'll catch on.

In our pursuit of connection, we've unintentionally turned "family time" into "family crime"—a crime against presence, against truly being there for one another. It's time to break free from the grip of our devices and the distractions they bring. We must reclaim those priceless moments that are slipping through our fingers.

Remember those 5 minutes. Protect those 5 minutes. Preserve those 5 minutes.

EMBRACING THE PRESENT

Ask yourself: Do *you* want it now or when *they're* gone? Do *they* want it now or when *you're* gone? The answer is obvious. Sorry to be so crass, but there's really no emotional upside in stockpiling the possessions of a dead person. Maybe one or two, but after that you're kind of getting Addams Family on me.

Instead, be a collector of time. A curator of time. A connoisseur of time. What truly matters is time—the time we spend with our loved ones, the memories we create, and the experiences we share.

Money cannot buy health, although it may provide temporary extensions. Money cannot buy time, although it may offer fleeting reprieves. The true richness of life lies in the moments we have, the connections we foster, and the love we share.

A CALL TO ACTION

As we navigate through the chapters of our lives, let us break free from the chains that shackle us. Let us embrace the journey, recognizing that there is no predetermined path. We may stumble and face hardships, but we also possess the resilience to adapt, grow, and find our way.

Don't waste your time or take it for granted. Cherish the moments we have, for they are the building blocks of a life well-lived.

THIS HOLIDAY PERIOD, WHY NOT GIVE THE GIFT OF TIME?

[Opening Scene: A family gathered around a holiday dinner table, faces illuminated by smartphone screens rather than the warm glow of candlelight. Voiceover kicks in.]

"This Holiday Period, why not give the gift of time? No, I'm not selling you a Rolex. I'm talking about memories, people!"

[Cut to: A mother placing her phone face-down and starting to carve the turkey.]

"It's laughable, really. We're more connected than ever, yet completely disconnected where it counts."

[Cut to: A teenager locking away his phone in a drawer and joining the family at the table.]

"Imagine a world where 'presence' isn't just an app notification. Earth-shattering, isn't it?"

[Cut to: The whole family playing board games, laughing together.]

FOREVER CHANGED

"Let's stop playing 'who texted me' bingo and start actually talking to each other!"

[Cut to: The camera pulls back to reveal the whole scene is a framed photo, with text overlay: **Invest in Memories, Not Megabytes**.]

"Visit www.foreverchanged.life for meaningful, phone-free gift ideas. Because if you're not careful, you might just reconnect with the ones you love."

"Give the gift of time, not just your Wi-Fi password. Because the best connection isn't measured in bars, it's measured in moments!"

[Ending Scene: Screen fades to black, displaying the website and slogan: **foreverchanged.life — Disconnect to Reconnect**.]

[End]

CHAPTER 6
HELLO I'M JOSEPH JAFFE AND I'M A TALK SHOW HOST

IF YOU WERE TO MEET JIMMY FALLON, JIMMY KIMMEL, OR STEPHEN Colbert, and before them, David Letterman or Jay Leno, and you had to ask them what they did for a living, they'd probably respond by saying, "I'm a talk show host."

Hi, there. My name is Joseph Jaffe. I'm a talk show host.

If you were to ask me today to describe myself or tell you what I did for a living, I would tell you that I am a talk show host.

To be honest, I'm not actually making a living from this.

That's kind of a joke. My wife is not laughing.

So maybe you should ask me, "What do I do for a life?"

I would say I'm a talk show host.

Hi, there. My name is Joseph Jaffe. I'm a talk show host.

Let me tell you what I'm not.

I'm not any of the things that I was before the pandemic - BP.

In order to be forever changed, you have to be changed forever.

> In order to be forever changed, you have to be changed forever.

FOREVER CHANGED

How can I prove that I'm forever changed? How about the fact *nothing* that I do today, or *nothing* that I'll do tomorrow is remotely reminiscent of my life before the world stood still.

So who was I before the pandemic?

BEFORE THE PANDEMIC, I WAS A CONSULTANT.

I was a member of the secret society known as the Chronic Consultants Guild or CCG for short.

As part of our mandate, we had to come up with a certain number of frameworks, 2x2 Matrices or acronyms every single year - otherwise we lost our membership and of course our secret handshake.

I consulted since I left the agency world in 2002.

At the time, I liked the idea of being a consultant. I always wanted to be a consultant. I always looked up to companies like Accenture, Deloitte, PwC, McKinsey, Bain, Booz Allen, BCG.

There was something magical about consulting that held a certain allure; never be tied down to one client at one time, the ability to demonstrate my agility, my versatility, to work on multiple pieces of businesses across multiple industries, across multiple geographies, solving big hairy audacious goals, objectives and challenges.

I got to flex my strategic chops during my agency life days. There were many unbelievably smart, talented strategic minds working in the agency business and besides, they loved the "British" accent (I'm South African), but at the end of the day, if to a hammer, everything's a nail, advertising agencies produce ads - they may tell you they don't, but that's what they do...they produce ads. No matter what the problem, the solution is almost always going to result in, "let's advertising our way out of this mess" and usually, it'll involve television advertising (see: Life after the 30-second spot)

CHAPTER 6 - HELLO I'M JOSEPH JAFFE AND I'M A TALK SHOW HOST

Strategy was a peculiar oddity insofar that the agency's clients expect the strategy thrown in as value add – kind of like unlimited salad and breadsticks at the Olive Garden.

So was the consulting world any better? Bigger; broader; focused on how the entire business works, the environment in which it operates, and the many moving parts and constituencies influenced and impacted by its actions. So essentially the horizontal yin to the agency world's vertical yang.

Can I be an equal opportunity offender? In the consulting world, your problem will take 2-3 years and cost well over seven figures before the recommendation to your tiny nail is one extremely large and lavish….hammer.

Sigh.

I guess the grass wasn't necessarily greener on the other side and then along came COVID and sprayed the entire lawn with weed killer. Or pee. Pick your metaphor.

BEFORE THE PANDEMIC, I WAS A THOUGHT LEADER.

I'll tell you that the term itself is a little maligned. It seems a little indulgent, I won't lie. It's self-designated or proclaimed, to be sure. For starters, there is no thought leader's society or guild. No certification. No acronym quota. And it's a bit fuzzy, shall we say, a bit ephemeral in terms of what it means to be a thought leader. But personally, I've always loved the term.

Thought leader: a leader in thought.

Well, I do that a lot. I think a lot. Sometimes I even get paid to think. And as someone who might stand up in front of thousands of people on a stage, facilitate workshops, coach leadership teams, contribute to a panel, or address a closed-door offsite, my job is to deliver thought or thinking. Some of it actually is quite good.

FOREVER CHANGED

Thinking from a leadership position.

So what is leadership?

Leadership implies being on top or in front or out in front. You can't be the leader of the pack when you are deferring to someone else in front of you. In some cases you can reference that or who came before you, benchmarking past and precedent, but when it comes to the present or the future, if you're a leader, you lead.

No real ambiguity here.

There are many ways to do that. But here are four very simple ways:

1. Come up with original thought (I'd like to think the premise and formula of Forever Changed is just that), or
2. Building on someone else's original content, generally another thought leader. If Malcolm Gladwell comes up with 3 rules of how to create a Tipping Point, have the audacity to submit a fourth. OK, that might be a little too bodacious. Here's a more grounded example: if someone comes up with 5 reasons why work-from-home is here to stay, come up with 5 more...
3. Put an original spin - your authentic take on something that already exists. As an example, if Simon Sinek introduces the idea of "Start with Why" offer your version of "Stop with Why" or "Start with When" or what "Start with Why" means for the education sector, which would most likely be your focus area or subject matter expertise.
4. Zig when the others are zagging. So, when there is a consensus (me-too) about a piece of news, opinion, or perspective, with everyone moving in one direction, **you move in the exact opposite direction**. Not only are you applying and providing your original take, but you are also coming up with a completely different take at

CHAPTER 6 - HELLO I'M JOSEPH JAFFE AND I'M A TALK SHOW HOST

that. Everyone thinks Elon sunsetting the Twitter brand name and rebranding it as X is essentially marketing suicide, you defend and justify why this makes sense, given Twitter's brand was already languishing and this move brings all of Musk's projects under one umbrella. To clarify, this isn't a license to be contrarian for the sake of it. I know enough dogmatic people out there. Think more Kafka and less Dafka.

Warning: "Professional Thought Leader - don't try this at home!"

Here's another example: If Seth Godin writes one of the world's most popular books called, "Permission Marketing," have the chutzpah to write your very first online article titled, "I'd rather beg for forgiveness than ask for permission."

I was the moron who wrote that article and Seth was the first comment on my article – literally seconds after I published it – ripping me a new one. It was almost my last article as well.

BEFORE THE PANDEMIC, I WAS A WRITER

Thought leaders tend to be writers.

Being a published author used to be a pretty big deal, but lately you just need to have purchased enough fake followers to get a deal and an advance. These days, you'll also need to commit to purchasing several thousand copies to get your guaranteed deal.

Pay to Play.

And it definitely favors the bigger players with deeper pockets. The corporations who will have no problem bankrolling a very elaborate calling card and then handing copies to every employee, as well as every client.

FOREVER CHANGED

Also, these books are most likely ghostwritten anyway or botwritten.

These days, anyone can be an author, because anyone can self-publish a book. Quite frankly anyone can self-write a book, thanks to generative-AI.

I'm all for the leveling of playing fields. I'm bullish on the democratization and monetization of publishing. I love offerings like Substack (jaffejuice.substack.com) and I'm watching the tokenization of publishing via blockchain very closely. I would have liked to have published this book on the blockchain, but the market is just not ready yet. I have however done something pretty landmark, which is to create a fractional ownership use case using this very book.

More on that later in the book...

Whilst I love the "leveling of playing fields" promise of self-publishing, I still think this should be done "the right way." I'm a big fan of the physicality of a book. Hardcover all the way, baby.

The thrill, and I mean it is a thrill, to walk into somebody's office and see your book on their bookshelf. Sometimes they don't even realize it's yours (probably because they didn't read it!), but when they do, there's an amazing lightbulb realization moment.

I've read your book. I've read your book five times. I've dog-eared your book and highlighted your book and recommended your book and bought your book for every one of my team...

It's a great feeling, even though you're not going to make any money from your book - at least not through the traditional route. It's the greatest resume virtue imaginable.

The ability to hand over your book with a personalized autographed message to a prospective client is one of the best ways to establish a baseline of credibility.

CHAPTER 6 - HELLO I'M JOSEPH JAFFE AND I'M A TALK SHOW HOST

Thought leaders should come with an established track record of "thought leadership" and should be able to carry a book, so much so that the self-publishing route should be able to go toe-to-toe with the old guard.

This is why I decided to self-publish my 6th book.

Let's see if I'm "write."

BEFORE THE PANDEMIC, I WAS A KEYNOTE SPEAKER

You don't make money from the royalties of your book when you go the traditional publisher route. You don't make it up in volume either, not unless you're Prince Harry. I ain't no prince.

You make it up on the speaking circuit.

For almost two decades, I racked up 50+ countries as I keynoted my way to every continent, but Antarctica. I said, "Call me!"

Many trips stand out, like the trip to Caracas, Venezuela. It was an unforgettable experience on so many levels.

I was there to deliver a three-hour seminar in front of a room with maybe 1000 people. The first session focused on my first book, "Life after the 30-second spot," and the second on my second book, "Join the Conversation." In-between was a 15-minute break where people could treat the pain with alcohol or attempt to stay awake with caffeine.

There was only one other speaker in the lineup, Philip Kotler. Professor Philip Kotler, my idol.

Turns out I had met him briefly before, but he would never have remembered. It was 1997, and I had just arrived in the US, thinking the smartest move to kick off my American adventure would be with an MBA. It would be a terrific way to assimilate, integrate, and learn the business culture; fast track context through an academic experience.

Spoiler alert: I never got in.

It was my second major "across the board" rejection (and not my last).

My first came in my final year at college when all the big brands like the Unilevers or Accentures of the world came a-knocking to campus to recruit the best and the brightest.

I was pretty much top of my class with a bunch of class medals to boot.

I never got a single callback.

In fact, I even started referring to my favorite interview clothing as my rejection suit.

Perhaps it was the weird maroon pants. Maybe that's why I got rejected. Who the hell wears maroon pants to a job interview?

You can't keep a good man down. I moved on to the greatest work experience anyone could hope or dream for. Nando's Chickenland. The Taste of Portugal. THE coolest, hippest brand in South Africa. For five years, I helped grow one of the most incredible brands in the world.

I arrived at Ellis Island (ok, JFK) ready to tell my interviewers how Nando's was not about chicken. It had never been about chicken. It was about passion, pride, courage, integrity, and most of all family. Our mission statement, which I had the privilege to help develop.

None of them gave a crap.

I applied at five colleges based on their brand recognition. Brand awareness. Marketing 101.

CHAPTER 6 - HELLO I'M JOSEPH JAFFE AND I'M A TALK SHOW HOST

Harvard. Wharton. NYU. Columbia. Kellogg, where Philip Kotler taught (so I had to apply there.)

Note to self: next time, have at least one safety school in your back pocket.

Once again, I went through a series of blanket rejections, although I did get one callback - NYU. And today, all these years later, I'm an adjunct, teaching there. The circle is complete.

Back to the Future: I flew to Chicago within the first two weeks of landing in the US. It was the end of March, and I'd never experienced cold like this in my life. Evanston was freezing. I wouldn't wish it on my worst enemy. Years later, I would tour the campus around the same time of year with my daughter and found it "crisp."

While I was there, one of the things I made sure to do was visit Philip Kotler's lecture. I sat at the back and watched like a good fan boy. Afterwards, I went and introduced myself to him. I might have thrown underwear at him (this actually happened to him in Caracas, albeit from females). The man is a legend. I vigorously shook his hand, and after the hundredth time and not letting go, I believe he called security.

Now back to Caracas.

There were only two speakers. Myself and Philip Kotler. I sent a message through our host to see if he would be open to meeting me. Would he like to meet me? Would he like to spend some time with me?

And the reply was that he would love to.

Now I have to tell you, I arrived a day earlier. Possibly two. Flying business class or maybe it was First. I needed to get in early to acclimate and get a good night's sleep. Very fragile. Very precious.

FOREVER CHANGED

Not Philip Kotler. Philip red-eyed in, the morning of the presentation. He went straight to his hotel room and took a quick power nap. And then he delivered a three-hour seminar de force that afternoon.

Right after that, he met me in a private penthouse bar. We sat for a couple of hours and chatted. Afterwards, we went to a lavish reception thrown by the PR agency overlooking this magnificent valley.

And then he went straight to the airport and promptly red-eyed back home.

And all the while, Philip and I were escorted by two-armed security guards with semi-automatic weapons. In fact, as we were driving in the armored vehicle, I decided to make conversation and asked the security guards what their next gig was.

They told me the next evening they were with Maroon 5. I kid you not. I was just thinking to myself, clearly you are being punished by the fact that you're hanging out with Joseph Jaffe the night before you're with Adam Levine.

After a good night's rest, I flew out the next day to Atlantis in the Bahamas for a corporate offsite. Don't cry for me, Venezuela.

Back to Philip in the Penthouse Bar.

This man in his late 70's or early 80's, who was on the ground for perhaps eighteen hours, now enduring two hours with yours truly.

Can you guess who did all the talking? And can you guess who did all the listening? And can you guess who took all the notes?

I talked. And I talked. And I talked.

Philip listened. Philip wrote. And Philip learned.

He taught me so much that day. You see, he was still learning. He hadn't stopped learning. He'll never stop learning.

CHAPTER 6 - HELLO I'M JOSEPH JAFFE AND I'M A TALK SHOW HOST

And I remember saying to him that I felt like such a fool while I was trying to impress him, and what could he possibly learn from me.

He told me not to feel bad and that he intended to use all my new-age intellectual property in his next book and take the credit for it. We both laughed.

A sense of humor as well? Is there anything this man can't do?

I had the pleasure of sitting down with him twice thereafter, including having him and Seth Godin on my show on my 50th Birthday, December 24th, 2020.

I think he actually did use my ideas in his next book, at least I hope he did.

Philip Kotler is a thought leader.

Philip Kotler is a writer.

Philip Kotler is a keynote speaker.

And guess what? I'm none of those.

At least not anymore.

I'm a talk show host.

CHAPTER 7
SIGNS

Once upon a time, there lived a man in a quaint two-story house near a river. Unfortunately, as fate would have it, the river began to flood, bringing with it impending danger. Various warnings were broadcasted through radio, TV, and shortwave frequencies. Large jeeps roamed the area, evacuating people to safety. As a jeep approached the man's house, the urgency in the rescuers' voices was evident.

"You are in grave danger! Your life is at stake. Please evacuate and let us help you," they pleaded.

But the man, standing firmly on his doorstep, held onto his faith. "Fear not," he replied confidently. "I have unwavering faith that I will be safe. The flood cannot harm me, for God will protect me."

Despite his conviction, the water continued to rise.

Eventually, the floodwaters forced him to retreat to the second floor of his house. A boat passed through the area and arrived at his doorstep. The rescuers, desperate to save his life, implored him to take action.

"You are in immediate danger! If you stay, you will drown. Please, come with us," they urged.

Yet he remained unperturbed. "No need to worry," he reassured them. "I have faith that everything will be fine. Even as the floodwaters rise, I believe God will take care of me."

Still, the flood persisted.

CHAPTER 7 - SIGNS

With the water level steadily climbing, the man sought refuge on the roof of his house. A helicopter pilot, spotting him from above, maneuvered the aircraft and hovered near him. Using a megaphone, the pilot pleaded with him to grab the rope ladder hanging just above his head.

"You are still in danger! The floodwaters continue to rise, and unless you grab the ladder, you will drown. Let us help you," the pilot exclaimed.

But the man, resolute in his faith, responded calmly, "Do not worry about me. Though the flood has grown higher, my faith remains unshaken. God will take care of me."

As the floodwaters reached their peak, the man tragically succumbed to the rising tides and drowned.

At the gates of heaven, the man confronted God with disappointment in his eyes. "I had faith in you, and yet you allowed me to perish," he lamented.

God replied, "I sent you a jeep, a boat, and a helicopter. What more could I have done for you?"

THE AWAKENING

Reflecting on the profound experience of the Global Pandemic, I couldn't help but wonder if we truly seized the opportunity it presented. Rather than dismissing it as a mere calamity, what if we embraced the lessons it taught us? Amidst the chaos and adversity—both good and bad—lurked an invaluable catalyst for personal growth and resilience. To let such an opportunity slip through our fingers would be a squandered gift.

THE SILENT MESSAGE

One cannot ignore the significance of a global pandemic, symbolized by the sight of people worldwide donning masks—everyone except those in red states! It seemed as if a higher power was silently urging us to practice humility and listen more attentively. Perhaps our narcissism, hedonism, self-absorption, and self-indulgence had veiled our ability to truly listen, drowning out the voices of others.

We often enter conversations armed with predetermined questions and firmly entrenched biases, whether in a business meeting, high school reunion, or Thanksgiving gathering. In my show, "Joseph Jaffe is not Famous," I take a different approach. I have no questions. I have no script. I have no show notes. All I do is invite my guests to volunteer three things they want to talk about, three things they want to promote and three fun facts about them. More often than not, we don't even make it through their 3 topics, which could be just a single word or two, Cognitive Dissonance, Adversity or Clarity. That's all I really need to power my Seated Soliloquy and fuel an entire hour of conversation. I find it indulgent, even arrogant, to assume I know my guests before they even sit down. I want them to tell their stories. By actively listening, I unearth hidden gems, insights, and magical moments that propel us into unexpected and thought-provoking discussions.

Most of the time, the real magic is in the dying moments of the conversation, and often times when the "camera isn't even rolling." It's the final words spoken that hold the greatest value and profundity. Sometimes, it's the result of a simple, throwaway question like, "Anything else you'd like to add?" It's in those unguarded moments, free from recording or formalities, that the truth pours out. And yet, we often cut those moments short, lose our focus because of artificial time constraints (hold that thought, we gotta take an advertising break,) and later regret our decision not to have allowed that conversation to continue.

There's method behind that madness and it's simpler than we think. Towards the end of a conversation – and especially when the director yells "cut" - people become less guarded and more relaxed.

CHAPTER 7 - SIGNS

Unburdened by formalities, they reveal their authentic selves. Or perhaps it's the power of asking open-ended questions that truly elicit genuine responses.

Did you know that listening and responding simultaneously is physiologically impossible, yet we find ourselves formulating our next retort as the person directly in front of us is still talking, instead of absorbing, internalizing, and empathizing. This perpetual cycle hinders our ability to find common ground, to truly connect. I should share that insight with Congress.

Excerpt from Dan Lyons' appearance on Joseph Jaffe is not Famous:

"There's a great story about Ruth Bader Ginsburg, and the clerks who worked for her who had to learn that when she seemed to finish speaking, she hadn't really finished; she was just stopping to think. And if you just jumped in as soon as she said her last word, in a way you were actually interrupting her. And so they developed this thing called The Mississippi rule, which is, when she stopped talking and before you talk, you go "One Mississippi, Two Mississippi," and if she still hasn't said anything, then it was safe to go ahead and say what you want to say. You can find those natural breaks..."

The face masks we wore during the pandemic silently implored us to listen, learn, **and then** respond. In that order. We are reminded of the saying, *"We have two ears and one mouth, so we should listen twice as much as we speak."* Yet, even when we use our ears, we often fail to truly listen and miss the signs that surround us.

I recently had an "intense" virtual coffee session in the Collective Cafe, where – thanks to a listener, Rhonda, who just wrote "listening intensely" in the chat box - I coined the phrase "intense listening." Consider intense listening one step beyond active listening. If you'd like to get a copy of this session and summary, please visit foreverchanged.life

FOREVER CHANGED

If we're honest with ourselves, we often care more about our own words than those of others. Arguments with our loved ones often stem from a self-centered perspective. If only we could truly listen, arguments might cease to exist.

One Mississippi. Two Mississippi.

Early in my personal journey, it was my wife who brought my listening deficiencies to light. One day, she stormed into my office, frustration etched on her face, and exclaimed, "Stop talking! You talk and you talk and you talk, you interrupt your guests, you talk over your guests. LET THEM TALK!"

Immediately, I dismissed her words, but deep down, I knew she was right (as always.) This began my transformation. During my show, I adopted an invisible mask, learning to silence myself. No ad breaks, no interruptions. Sometimes, guests spoke uninterrupted for minutes, even ten minutes. I think the record is around 15. It took immense self-control to restrain myself from interjecting, but I never said a word which is not to say I wasn't digging my fingernails into my skin to the point of drawing blood.

I'm still working on this skill. I think I'll be working on it for the rest of my life.

And the most astonishing outcome was that people began to relax, to open up. They shared intimate stories, confessing, "I've never told anyone this before" or "I promised myself I wouldn't cry." I was becoming Barbara Walters, rest in peace.

And the crowning glory, "you're such a good listener."

I just threw up a little in my mouth right now.

This became a pivotal moment in my personal growth. It should serve as a reminder for all of us to be less narcissistic, more selfless, and more generous. It's time to pay it forward, to embrace the karma that the world desperately needs.

How do I know this to be true? The answer lies in the signs, particularly the glaring sign of the Global Pandemic. But were we paying attention? Were **you** paying attention?

Have we allowed ourselves to be changed forever by this extraordinary event? If not, should we consider making a change? Do we sense the need for transformation? Denial only leads to self-deception.

THE INVISIBLE SIGN

During the pandemic, opportunists emerged, capitalizing on the adage, "Never let a good crisis go to waste." From price gouging hand sanitizers to entrepreneurs exploiting rapid tests and even the social audio app Clubhouse, where self-help gurus, overnight coaches and good old-fashioned scammers peddled their wares, it became clear that many were missing the opportunity.

Instead of wasting this moment (there's still time!), I implore you to seize the opening to transform your own life.

Just as the man in the story earlier failed to recognize the signs of divine intervention, we often overlook the signs right in front of us, treating them as if they were invisible. As the lyrics of Ace of Base's song go, "I saw the sign, and it opened up my eyes." But did we truly see the signs? Are our eyes open to the possibilities and the potential for a new, purposeful path?

JIMINY CRICKET

Amid my mother's ongoing battle with cancer, I had to make an incredibly important decision.

Pain management had taken precedence over treatment, indicating a transition from mid-life to end of life. I traveled to South Africa to visit her, always wondering if this would be the last time I would see her.

A friend who had experienced a similar loss urged me to go as many times I was able (it still wasn't enough), emphasizing that being there while she was relatively stable would allow for more meaningful conversations. And so, I embarked on the journey multiple times.

On the very first morning of one of my visits, I woke up from my jet lagged slumber and walked to the family room where my mother spent most of her days shackled to her lay-z-boy, contemplating her existence. She motioned for me to sit down and assured me there was no need to panic. Cue the panic. Earlier that morning, she had experienced a "minor fall" while attempting to avoid a power outage. South Africa was cursed with "loadshedding" multiple times a day. Turns out there's not enough electricity to power the homes of the corrupt politicians, let alone their constituents. Where is Elon when you need him?

The culprit and catalyst for the fall: a cricket.

In 47 years of living in that house, my mother had never encountered a cricket—inside or outside. It was a sign. I shared with her my belief that the cricket was a manifestation of my late father, warning her about the perils of falling in her fragile state and living alone. I urged her to take more precautions, such as using Life Alert.

The incident served as a wake-up call. The fracture in my mother's hip was non-displaced, which meant not requiring invasive action. It necessitated a realization that she needed to be more cautious while living alone. It was a sign for her to consider live-in assistance and to prioritize her safety.

CHAPTER 7 - SIGNS

While I contemplated the significance of the cricket and looked forward to having a meaningful dialog with my late father, our housekeeper crushed it with her heel and silenced the messenger for good.

When I look back on it now, it might have been a different sign altogether. The fall accelerated her immobility and ultimately, she succumbed to Cancer in January of 2023. The sign was actually not hers at all. She was in such pain that her inevitable death was a massive pain relief as much I hate to admit it.

So who's sign was it? I think we all know the answer to that.

I just got goosebumps.

THE SIGNS WE CHOOSE TO IGNORE

In moments of triumph or despair, we often resort to blaming or thanking a higher power. Perhaps those are the times we actively look for signs, but how many other life-changing signs do we truly notice when we're not actively looking, or miss altogether?

 To acknowledge a sign is to attribute it to cosmic, spiritual, karmic, or religious forces; serendipity or even just luck of the draw, but ultimately acknowledging that things happen for a reason. This rings especially true in the case of a global pandemic—an undeniable sign. And if we dare to consider it as a random coincidence, the implications would be far more terrifying.

Randomness is insignificance and we are not insignificant. We matter. You matter. You are part of a gargantuan, cosmic tapestry and without your tiny piece of string, it will all unravel catastrophically. You are a glorious butterfly. When you die, there is a void in the world; there is an absence of goodness; there is a hole in the universe. This is not my opinion. It's mystical. It's religious.

Ironic right? Steve Jobs lived to create a dent in the universe, but it is only in death that we actually break through.

> Steve Jobs lived to create a dent in the universe, but it is only in death that we actually break through.

So, how does this differ from being laid off or experiencing other clear signs? The pandemic presented a unique opportunity for *collective empathetic introspection*. Unlike isolated events that affect only a few, this crisis affected us all simultaneously. It evoked shared experiences, allowing us to relate, empathize, and learn. Yet, as we reflect, some of us have taken action, while others have not.

Believing that every experience has led us to this very moment, we must ask ourselves, "If today were our last day, would our lives have made a difference?" The answer should always be, "hell yeah."

Let us not waste this crisis. Let us not ignore the signs. Instead, let us embrace the opportunity to start anew, to embark on a journey of personal transformation. Regardless of age or circumstance, it is never too late to begin, to redirect our lives towards purpose and meaning.

THE AWAKENING

Change is seldom easy, often accompanied by pain. That is why we tend to overlook the signs that are right in front of us. We rationalize, defend, and deny what is obvious, clinging to what is familiar and comfortable. We give second chances to those who have let us down, hoping they will change, while compromising our own well-being.

The change has to come from within. Don't wait for others to change. Change yourself.

It is time to open our eyes and wake up from this trance of complacency. Early warning signs are not always hidden; perhaps they never are. They are often times hiding in plain sight. They can be

CHAPTER 7 - SIGNS

as clear as day if we are willing to pay attention. It is so important to establish personal checkpoints in our lives – both professional and personal - to create a customized and personalized set of early warning signs for relationships, careers, and overall well-being.

For those trapped in miserable jobs, feeling frustrated and unfulfilled, it is the clearest sign that change is needed. But what does that change look like? And why do we only notice the signs in the rear-view mirror? What would need to be true to break free from the handcuffs of unhappiness? How do we gauge personal and professional growth? Are we truly learning, evolving, and moving towards a life of fulfillment?

Perhaps one approach is to imagine ourselves in the future, looking back at the path we have taken or the one we are yet to take. What did we achieve? What did we contribute? How will we be remembered? These reflections can guide us in recognizing the signs that indicate we are on the right track or veering off course. Positive prophesizing is a great way to identify what went right, why it went right, and then all we need to do is to take action. Easier said than done I know.

Regular mental health check-ins are crucial as well. Taking clarity breaks, moments to pause, slow down, and assess our emotional well-being allows us to stay on course and make necessary adjustments. Otherwise, we are flying blind, without a clear sense of direction.

Let us create our own sign language, a personalized guidebook filled with tips, tools, tricks, indicators, rubrics, litmus tests for relationships, careers, and life. This way, we can't; we won't let the signs pass us by, unnoticed and unheeded.

We must acknowledge that blame-shifting and evading responsibility is a futile exercise. When faced with signs and opportunities for change, we must take ownership of our lives. It is tempting to relinquish control, to attribute our inaction to external circumstances or the actions of others. But the power to transform lies within us.

Personal responsibility is empowering and liberating, especially in a safe, blameless environment.

As we navigate a world plagued by crises and injustices, we must resist the urge to turn a blind eye. We cannot overlook the signs that demand our attention, but we also mustn't get overwhelmed and debilitated by the sheer weight of the world on our tiny, teeny shoulders. We need to be selfish without being selfish if you get what I mean. Change begins right in front of your face.

Focus on what we can control—the choices we make, the actions we take. By doing so, we become agents of change, contributing to a better world.

So, I implore you, let the signs guide you. Embrace the opportunity to start anew, to awaken to your true potential. The world needs your unique voice, your empathy, and your ability to make a difference. Let the signs be your compass, leading you on a transformative journey.

Remember, it is never too late to start. Today is the day to take that first step, to embrace the signs, and to forge a path that is aligned with your purpose and values. Seize the opportunity and become forever changed. The choice is yours.

CHAPTER 8
ANATOMY OF A SHOW

DO YOU REMEMBER WHEN IT ALL BEGAN?

I remember the early days of COVID. In the US, it followed a familiar path that aligned with previous scares like H1N1 and Swine Flu. At that time, I was on my way to South Africa to see my mom. Cases were already emerging in New York, there was an outbreak around the corner from me in New Rochelle, and who could forget *Party Zero* in Westport, Connecticut, which by the way involved literally every one of my family and friends. There was a run on masks, hand sanitizer, and wipes. I managed to pick up travel-size hand sanitizers from a gas station and a doctor friend secured a couple of face masks that "fell off the back of a truck." The thrill of life on the run.

I flew with a stopover in London, where COVID effects were a little more visible than in the US. My first stop was to see my best friend at his office. We didn't shake hands or hug; instead, we tapped our ankles in a somewhat joking manner, not fully convinced of the necessity. I was extra cautious because of my mother's underlying condition.

Several days later, my friend tested positive for COVID.

Looking back, it was so obvious he was shedding the virus, especially considering his recent trip to – wait for it - Northern Italy, the epicenter of the European outbreak. Talk about missing – or rather ignoring - the signs!

Afterwards, I took a couple of business meetings, engaging in various greetings from handshakes to fist bumps. At that point, I was

FOREVER CHANGED

using hand sanitizer after every shake or bump. Masks were sporadic.

Next, I visited my sister, hugging and kissing her hello and goodbye. She also ended up testing positive for COVID shortly after, likely contracting it from my friend. Avoiding the tube, I did take the Heathrow Express back to the airport. I wore a mask, but it kept on fogging up my glasses and so I took it off.

The rest of the trip was uneventful. South Africa was even more relaxed than the UK. Being at the foot of Africa does have its perks.

The night before I was due to fly back, I was keynoting at Adele Searll's 100 Club, an organization focused on Networking, Business and Philanthropy, and one my mom was heavily involved in. Just before I was meant to speak, the phone rang. It was my wife – who had been at Party Zero – letting me know that she felt a little *under the weather*. Cough, headache, scratchy throat…probably nothing.

She never gets sick.

You do know you probably have COVID, right?

I flew back to the US and upon landing in London, I received notifications that the administration had implemented a travel ban, creating uncertainty about my return. Luckily, US citizens and permanent residents were still allowed back into the country.

I may have passed my wife on the I-95 highway, as she was heading to get tested. Testing was not readily available at the time. I knew I would most likely enter a minimum 14-day quarantine, and I figured it was inevitable I would get COVID as I was living in the same house as my wife, assuming she was positive…which she was. Before entering the house, I stocked up on groceries (and by groceries I mean toilet rolls), uncertain about the availability in the near future.

CHAPTER 8 - ANATOMY OF A SHOW

I isolated myself in the guest suite on the third floor for about three weeks, which I jokingly referred to as marriage. Surprisingly, I never contracted COVID, nor did my kids. My wife wore her mask whenever she was around us and even cooked with gloves on. During this time, packages from Amazon were left untouched for 48-72 hours to allow any potential virus to dissipate, followed by thorough disinfection.

I became obsessed with CNN, watching Governor Cuomo's briefings and the White House Task Force updates. The ticker crawl, displaying infection numbers, hospitalizations, deaths, and recoveries, captured my attention. Meanwhile, my speaking and consulting engagements started getting canceled one after another, leaving me with no work. The cupboard was bare.

Amidst the panic, I realized that everyone was in the same boat, which oddly calmed me. Peers in the industry were discussing strategies and figuring out what to do. I attended a webinar with other speakers, and the consensus was clear: upgrade equipment, buy a ring light and webcam, and update websites to emphasize virtual offerings. They were zigging, but I decided to zag.

Feeling a subconscious urge to record my experiences, I started doing Facebook Live sessions to connect with others and share my thoughts and observations. The live streaming was new to me. My only previous video experience was 10 years prior with JaffeJuiceTV. Even though I've been told I have a "face for radio," I did another Facebook Live session the next day. And another the following day. It became a routine—rinse and repeat.

On the third day, I managed to get a COVID test at a local school. I documented the experience on Facebook Live, driving down our town's Post Road that resembled Christmas or Thanksgiving Day. The sound of sirens in the distance reminded me of a scene from

FOREVER CHANGED

"The Walking Dead." It was eerie to say the least. Facebook Live became a daily ritual.

Soon after, I decided to transition to a new platform: Zoom. I appreciated the ability to simulcast the stream on Facebook or YouTube and the functional upgrades it offered, like sharing my screen with a PowerPoint slide deck or visiting essential websites. I wanted to inject creativity and personality into my broadcasts, making them more engaging.

Unbeknownst to me, I was taking a significant step toward launching my talk show.

Then, during a conversation with my sister in London - still battling COVID - she shared her business pivot: transitioning her spinning studio into a live and on-demand streaming at-home solution. This involved her loading and unloading heavy bikes onto a U-Haul and dropping them off at her customers' homes. Inspired by her resilience, I invited her as a "guest" on my "show" to tell her story. Sharon became Guest #1 and delivered a fantastic interview. I couldn't have been prouder, and it was thanks to that interview that she and her business partner, Hils, who has since passed away from the same awful disease that took my mom (Cancer 3 Humans 0,) received media coverage in a prominent newspaper.

And so, CoronaTV was born. I was poking the bear. I liked the idea of pushing boundaries, finding hope, positivity, and optimism in a time of despair. Maybe, just maybe, I could be a counter-trend during these troubled times. Perhaps Corona Beer would buy into the idea or sponsor it (that didn't pan out, but I hear Bud Light is available!) I loved the idea of being a mouthpiece for business, marketing and entrepreneurship - celebrating its successes and being a cheerleader for creativity, innovation, and growth.

It struck me then and still does today, that there isn't a single business TALK show on television, dedicated to creativity, culture, in-

CHAPTER 8 - ANATOMY OF A SHOW

novation, leadership, and diversity. I firmly believe and I manifest this vision, position and responsibility, and that I am that person. I am that host.

Then one day I stumbled on a Facebook friend's "show" (everyone was streaming during those days) on Facebook. It was a revelation—production quality that rivaled or surpassed anything I had seen online or even television. Banners, tickers, overlays, logos, live comments—it had the engagement and life that even traditional talk shows lacked. Intrigued, I reached out to him, hoping he would share his secret sauce, but kind of expecting he wouldn't. He graciously and nonchalantly just said, "sure man...I'm using StreamYard."

StreamYard became a game-changer for me. Streamyard changed my life. Its capabilities allowed me to innovate, pivot, and iterate rapidly. From Facebook to Zoom to StreamYard, I had transformed my approach **in just three weeks**. It was a whirlwind of change, but it felt invigorating.

And with that, a show was truly born.

THE REBRAND

If I didn't have enough adversity and challenges to overcome, there was the additional obstacle of Google, YouTube, and the other social media platforms *miscategorizing* a show about hope, positivity, and optimism as one about rhetoric, partisan debates, and sensitive material. I was being shadow banned while trying to promote my show. Campaign rejection upon rejection, I couldn't understand what I was doing wrong.

Then it hit me, and I'm sure it hit you too. The name of the show: CoronaTV. Just the fact that I called it CoronaTV was enough to essentially get me blacklisted. I tried everything to outsmart the algorithm, removing the mention of CoronaTV from my intro, but

FOREVER CHANGED

I still faced restrictions due to *shocking events* (that's how Google referred to it), *sensitive topics, and even accusations of promoting alcohol to minors*. A double whammy. I even had to brief my guests, asking them not to mention anything related to Corona, COVID, pandemic, global pandemic (I would refer to it on air as the Global Patricia...maybe Karen would have been better?), vaccines, politics, or even drinking. It seemed like I needed a stiffer drink than a beer after all of that.

I recall a conversation with Bruce Turkel, a previous guest on my show.

Sidebar: Bruce is one of the nicest guys on the planet and someone I now have the privilege to call a friend. Just before COVID hit, I was being considered for a keynote speech in Peru. I was thrilled at the prospect of visiting Peru, a country I had always wanted to explore and where I hadn't yet spoken. We negotiated the fee, and I even proposed a partial barter arrangement, suggesting a VIP excursion to Cusco for a reduced fee. I requested that my wife be flown in as well. They agreed to include flying in my wife and a private tour of Machu Picchu in the package.

I didn't get the gig. I wasn't selected for the speaking engagement. They chose someone else. I experienced loss. But one thing I've learned from dealing with rejection - which happens frequently as an entrepreneur - is to always ask why and seek feedback. It's an opportunity to learn, retool, rethink, evolve, and improve for the next time. In this case, it wasn't about the fee; it was simply because they chose a better man instead; or in the absence of one, they settled for Bruce Turkel (I told you we are now friends!) I had never heard of Bruce before, and he had never heard of me.

But let me tell you, every one of you should know Bruce Turkel.

So, one day, I reached out to him and invited him to be on the show. Although complete strangers, he graciously accepted. We had an

CHAPTER 8 - ANATOMY OF A SHOW

> *incredible time, sharing fantastic chemistry and even doing Scooby-Doo impressions. Afterwards, I shared the backstory with him off-air. Ironically the gig was cancelled for him, because...you know. He has since appeared on my show multiple times, offered to host my son in Miami and we've even met IRL.*

Bruce mentioned something that hit me hard. *"You know, you're going to have to change the name of your show, right?"* I pondered it, wondering if it was necessary. Bruce's words struck a chord, especially when he said, *"It's like calling the show '9/11 TV.'"* My head dropped. My heart sank. He was absolutely right.

Bruce graciously offered to help me rebrand the show, asking probing questions about my vision, mission, North Star, and what motivated me. I shared with him that the show was never about me; it was about my guests. It was about helping people who were stuck at home or stuck in general. It was about supporting my fellow speakers, colleagues, and peers in the business, providing them with a platform, content strategy, and even sharing the show files afterward with them. I praised them effusively, sometimes excessively, as my wife would point out. She'd say, *"Stop kissing up to them. You're overly complimentary."* And she was right, as always. But I had a strong desire to lift them up and celebrate them, giving them that hour of video content they could cut, slice, dice, revise, upload, optimize, and use to benefit their businesses and brand. Rather than hiring someone and overpaying for specific video footage for their sizzle reels, I wanted to offer it to them for free.

Bruce and I continued our exploratory conversation and brainstorming, and I told him. *"If I ever have the fortune of having a manager or an agent representing me, and they decline an opportunity for me to be on someone else's podcast or show, I would fire them on the spot."* I love being the first guest on a new podcast with zero viewers or listeners, lending my name and IP. I share the appearance on all my social networks because I firmly believe in the concept of a rising tide floating all boats.

Bruce immediately lit up and started doodling something with his artistic flair. He announced, *"The name of your show is 'Joseph Jaffe is not Famous.'"* I instantly loved it. No lizard brain could talk me out of it. No overthinking or second-guessing. Joseph Jaffe is not Famous…**but my next guest is!**

I'm immensely grateful to Bruce for that discovery and the beautiful gift he gave me on that day.

CHAPTER 9
THE BUSINESS MODEL OF LIFE

THE BUSINESS MODEL OF LIFE IS BROKEN.

In Built to Suck, I wrote that the Business of Model of (Big) Business is Broken.

> *My contention, and a central part of the hypothesis of this book, is that corporations are terminal. They are diseased, and stand little to no chance of survival.*
>
> *The central operating system that powers the corporation, and will ultimately be its downfall, is SIZE. Scale, economies of scale, and the cost efficiencies of mass production that served as catalysts for the original growth engine are now backfiring. Size is no longer a growth enabler; it's a growth inhibitor.*
>
> *It has caused corporations to lose their edge—specifically their competitive edge. They are no longer equipped to adapt. To evolve. To change. They are simply too big and bureaucratic; too risk-averse and political.*
>
> *They proudly crow about their 100+ years of history; their founder(s) who are almost always white males; their mission statement, which invariably mentions the word "market leader" or "leadership." They fail to recognize that their days are most certainly numbered. They are rudderless, and lost at sea.*
>
> *Their inability to morph or pivot has put them on life support.*
>
> *The very size of companies and their desperate need for enormity and scale has become a vicious cycle spiraling downward toward inevitable doom.*

My inspiration or context for this assertion was to refer to big companies as "The Corporate Empire" and compare them to every other Empire that has – without fail or exception – gone the same way. The way of the dodo.

The lifespan of empires or civilizations is a topic that's been dissected by historians, economists, and social scientists for decades, and while there's no one-size-fits-all answer, Sir John Glubb's seminal work, "The Fate of Empires," suggested a life cycle of about 250 years or ten generations, consisting of phases such as the Age of Pioneers, the Age of Conquests, the Age of Commerce, and ultimately, the Age of Decadence.

BNY Mellon is the oldest Fortune 500 company currently at 239 years old (founded in 1784 by Alexander Hamilton.) Tick tock. Tick tock.

If you're interested in this topic, I'd recommend researching Diseconomies of Scale, Gigantism, Creative Destruction or just read Built to Suck.

THE BUSINESS MODEL OF LIFE IS BROKEN.

We spend our entire lives hoarding possessions - we hoard things, we hoard money, we hoard status. We hoard business cards. We hoard awards and trophies. And when we leave this earth, we leave all of that behind to a bunch of self-entitled, ungrateful squabbling kids, or in some rare cases, to a cat, or cats plural.

What's the point?

And the trophies and possessions are either sold at auction, eBay or a yard sale.

What's the point?

To illustrate this, I'm going to use a very famous retailing riddle that is used to teach about planning, projections, ordering, stocking, and so on.

CHAPTER 9 - THE BUSINESS MODEL OF LIFE

It's the day after Thanksgiving, and a supermarket owner walks into their store to inspect the number of turkeys—fresh and/or frozen. How many turkeys do they hope to find there? Do you know the answer?

You would think the answer would be zero. But you would be wrong.

Why? Because at zero, you have no idea how many disappointed customers there would have been. You have no idea whether one or 100 people came in to buy their turkeys only to leave empty-handed.

The answer isn't 100 either. Because that would represent inefficient ordering, food spoiling, shelves not being optimally stocked and the opportunity cost of not replacing the turkeys with other items.

The correct answer in fact is one - a single turkey - because one turkey represents one missed opportunity.

One turkey represents the fact the supermarket owner ordered just one too many. That's as close to perfect as you could ever get.

By the same token, **when we leave this earth, we should leave with one dollar to our name.**

> when we leave this earth, we should leave with one dollar to our name.

One dollar to our name because that would represent a life well-lived and a life well-loved.

It would represent a life where we were able to take what we earned and *invest* or spend it on ourselves, our loved ones, our family; maximizing our every moment and opportunity to turn those moments into memories. To completely, wholly and unabashedly embrace the connections, the relationships, the experiences that we were able to partake in.

FOREVER CHANGED

Think about it. Think about how you're approaching life.

Think about when you spend, when you save, when you hoard, when you choose not to spend.

Clearly, this is not a lesson in financial planning. If so, I'm the last person you should ever take advice from.

But it is a lesson in perspective. It is a lesson in being able to recognize how fragile life can be, how unpredictable life can be. You can be here today and gone tomorrow. And when you leave, the only person you need to be accountable to, to report to, and to be able to reconcile and come to peace with, is yourself.

Did you make the most of your time? Did you make the most of your opportunities? Did you repay the gift of life with the things that money can't buy...relationships?

And please DO trust me when I tell you that leaving a bunch of money to your kids is the most selfish thing you can do because it denies them. It strips them of the ability to earn, to struggle, to be challenged, to overcome adversity, to be able to realize the same successes, the same achievements, the same accomplishments that you did.

We always say that our goal is to give our kids the things that we never had. But the best thing to give your kids are LITERALLY the things that you never had — nothing. Give them the same opportunity. In fact, the best thing you can ever give them would be the lessons, the wisdom, the experience, the shortcuts, the hacks. Those lessons are invaluable - priceless gifts that money cannot buy.

It took a global pandemic for many people to realize that. It took a global pandemic for me to realize that. I hope it takes a global pandemic for you to realize that for you to recognize, even years later as it starts to fade in the rearview mirror, the importance of perspective and prioritization.

CHAPTER 9 - THE BUSINESS MODEL OF LIFE

CARPE VITAM / SEIZE LIFE

We're constantly looking beyond our noses; beyond our stomachs; beyond our stares for something bigger, something better.

We always look.

We can't help but covet.

We can't help but look at other people's lives and think, *"must be nice."*

Must be nice to be you.

Must be nice to have that job. That house. That boat.

Must be nice to have bought low and sold high.

Why don't we think it can be us? Why do we think it'll never happen to us.

It'll never be me.

I'll never write a book.

I'll never run a marathon.

I'll never sell out my collection.

Of course, it will. Of course, you will. Of course, I will.

It just might take time. Or a twist or two.

Can you see the signs - really SEE them; recognize them for what they are and what they represent?

What they represent is a gift, and based on a positive outlook on life, and a belief where your *Sage* prevails over your *Saboteur*, the gift – known or unknown; revealed or hidden; immediate or deferred – is yours and only yours to discover. In many instances, the gift is Movement. Forward Movement. Growth. Return to Growth.

Go on...TAKE ACTION!

BLIND TO THE SIGN / ZOOMING OUT

What if that sign is right in front of you, so close that you can almost touch it? So close that you can't see it. You're in the weeds. You are the devil in the details. The minutia has blinded you to the magnificence of possibility.

During COVID, I was on one of my regular Westport runs listening to Howard Stern interviewing Jerry Seinfeld. I remember the exact place that I was, for some reason, this insight, and so many insights that I've heard, I can map almost to the square inch where I was standing. Jerry was talking about zooming out in order to recognize and realize the bigger picture. And it absolutely resonated with me, so much so, that it is all over this book.

This is precisely why zooming out becomes essential—the first step towards a transformative journey. It's a process and we must be mindful not to zoom out excessively, to the point where we feel insignificant or lose sight of ourselves entirely.

To truly understand who we are and what we can become, we need to find balance and step out of our own bodies. Consider it an extraordinary out-of-body experience, where we observe ourselves objectively. Let this exploration reveal the depth of your potential and shape your vision for the future.

ZOOMING IN: REFLECTING ON THE DAY-TO-DAY

Now, let's shift our focus to the day-to-day aspects of your life, but what happens when we zoom in too much? When you are inside your body and inside your mind (head trash anyone?), you cannot see yourself directly or objectively. It is only through the reflection in a mirror that you catch a literal glimpse of who you are. But here's the rub: the reflection is not an exact representation. It can be distorted, leaving us to question if we truly see the real version of ourselves. What if the mirror is warped? What if it's cracked, skewing our perception?

CHAPTER 9 - THE BUSINESS MODEL OF LIFE

LENSES AND FILTERS: SHAPING PERSPECTIVES

Our perspectives are heavily influenced by the lenses and filters we use, with social media being a prime example. We see ourselves differently from how the world perceives us. Understanding this dynamic helps us navigate the complex interplay between self-perception and external judgment.

Comparing ourselves to others has obvious pitfalls. While role models are important, we need to avoid the pitfalls of *referential purgatory* especially when *objects in the social media mirror may appear very different from reality.* I don't know about you, but I have plenty of family photos, where we're all smiling like the perfect family, but seconds before we were at each other's throats.

"Seriously mom, this is the last @#$%^& photo you take of us on this vacation!"*

Here's a quick tip about comparisons. Be like the judges in the Olympic Games. Eliminate the highest and lowest score. Cut out the extremes. Find the average. Find your balance. Find your sweet spot.

If you should be fortunate enough to see Hamilton on Broadway, you'll want to avoid sitting in the nosebleed seats, but at the same time you won't want to occupy the front row either, unless of course you enjoy watching the spit expectorated from King George's mouth. One represents zooming out too much and the other zooming in excessively. Each directionally offers a unique experience, but the key lies in discovering something in-between - your own personal and unique equilibrium. It's about defining your own measures of success, breaking free from comparisons, and embracing the path that aligns with your true self.

Orchestra Section. Row J. Center

VERY WELL OFF

I never understood the concept of generational wealth until recently. First of all, back home in South Africa, my friends use two terms or phrases that are euphemisms in of themselves. One is, if you hear someone say, that person is well off, what it means is that their children will never have to work again. When you hear them say that person is *very* well off, that means their grandchildren will never have to work again. Now, for the most part, I guess we're talking about 1% of 1% of 1%, which will not apply to pretty much most of you reading this book, myself included.

WEALTH AS A BLESSING OR CURSE

What does it mean when your children will never have to work again? Is it a blessing? Or is it a curse? I am leaning towards it being a curse. When we want to give our children what we never had, why does this translate into money? It should be everything BUT wealth, at least not wealth that is measured and quantified in the form of money.

THE IMPORTANCE OF OPPORTUNITY

What we should strive to give them is opportunity. And this opportunity should not be a function of money or wealth, also known as privilege. Instead consider a function of learning, wisdom and if there's going to be access, let it be access to mentors. It's primarily about giving them opportunity. If we reflect on why generations of dreamers have set sail across the ages, often times undertaking the most dangerous or perilous journeys to the United States of America, we always see a common thread. Whether it's crossing treacherous oceans on barely sea-worthy rafts from Cuba or navigating dangerous terrain paying questionable individuals life savings to be smuggled across the Mexican border or fleeing persecution like the Pogroms in Russia and Eastern Europe, as many Jews did, the fact is, everybody migrated to the United States in pursuit of a better life.

CHAPTER 9 - THE BUSINESS MODEL OF LIFE

Not necessarily - and perhaps not especially - for themselves, but for their children. They weren't only in pursuit of wealth, but for things that money couldn't buy, and things that money cannot measure. Safety, security, peace of mind, opportunity, freedom from persecution, and the list continues. That's when giving our children what we never had lands. Freedom. Freedom of Choice. Free Choice. Peace. Peace of Mind.

REIMAGINING GENERATIONAL WEALTH

Generational wealth isn't about leaving money behind for the next generation. It's about being able to enable, empower, and position generations to come in a better situation than you encountered. And again, that boils down to opportunity. That relates to continuity. That comes down to the ability to ensure that if something were to happen to you, God forbid, something tragic, something sudden, something overnight, that your child, your grandchild, your business partner, your friend would be okay.

That they would have the tools needed and necessary to be okay.

Give a man a fish, you feed him for a day. Teach a man to fish, you feed him for a lifetime. Give him access to Chef Nobu Matsuhisa and he'll turn that pond into an empire.

EMBRACING MORTALITY

COVID changed the lives of so many people at a moment's notice. And I want to use this moment to emphasize the importance of having your affairs in order. Having a last will and testament, a living will. Considering life insurance, having a life insurance policy. You should be liberated by the fact that your affairs are in order. You should be emboldened by the fact you've taken care of all the dirty work, all the grunt work, all the ugly stuff, all the stuff we don't want to talk about; that we sweep under the rug. And let's be clear. This is not fun stuff.

Nor is imagining a day when you are no longer here, but hard as it is, I want to encourage you to take a moment to confront your own mortality; immerse yourself in your fragility; embrace the inevitability that this project known as your life *will* come to an end at some point in time. And rather than lament it, revel in it. Take pride in it. Because once you do, it's liberating.

Rather than commiserate it, celebrate it. Celebrate it by making sure that the next generation is in a position to pick up the ball and run with it. Continue your family's legacy, which is ultimately *their* legacy - keep the story going.

PONDERING LIFE'S INEVITABILITY

So many people are in denial. Denial is not a river on Egypt. I am probably one of them. Can you imagine life without your spouse? Can you think about life without a parent? Can you comprehend life without yourself? The thought of not being around for your loved ones or you is difficult to contemplate.

I became an orphan at 52. It's still tough to catch myself as I'm about to call my mom to tell her good news. Or that the new season of Yellowstone is now streaming. Or just calling her during the quiet times. The overwhelming emotion is pure loneliness. I feel so alone. There's no one to give me the answers and tell me what to do, even if – as it transpires – my mom was probably as clueless as I am.

THE HEDONISTIC LIFE

When I encourage people to live every day like it's their last day; their only day; their **BEST** day, I'm not really addressing the narcissists, who don't give a crap about anyone but themselves. That's the other extreme. When you live every single day as if it was your only or last day, without any care, concern or consideration for anyone else but yourself, well that's the bad kind. That's the selfish, the bad kind. That's clearly not what we're talking about here, and not what we're advocating here.

CHAPTER 9 - THE BUSINESS MODEL OF LIFE

HUMILITY OVER HUBRIS.

To be honest, I'm not sure people that live the narcissistic or hedonistic lifestyle are in fact living every day like it's their only day or their last day, because if they *were* living every day as if it was their only and last day, they would not be making it about themselves. They would be Oskar Schindler coming to terms with the life they led or the life they could have led. Instead of celebrating everything they did, they would be commiserating everything they didn't do or could have done.

That scene in Schindler's List. When Liam Neeson who plays Okcar Schindler looks at his wedding band, and realizes that he could have saved one more life. That whatever he did was still not enough. It's never enough. It's a contradiction of sorts. When you realize and recognize that whatever you do in this world will never be enough. And yet, and yet, you have to do it anyway. It shouldn't deter you. It shouldn't delay you. It shouldn't bog you down. It shouldn't depress you. Understanding, recognizing, and accepting your limitations is the first step towards living the forever changed life.

EMBRACING INSIGNIFICANCE

The ultimate humility. When you realize you're not the shit; that you're one small piece of an elaborate puzzle; one small cog in a much larger machine. But that piece, however small, and however many pieces there are in the puzzle; that cog, no matter how small, no matter how large or intricate, or complex, the machine is, is still an integral part of the equation. Without it, the puzzle is incomplete. Without it, the machine doesn't work because it's missing a key component. That's the great contradiction here. When you come to terms with how insignificant you are - this tiny, little speck, and yet, without you there is a conspicuous imperfection that cannot be filled by anyone but yourself.

Perfectly imperfect.

CONTEMPLATING PURPOSE

Whether the purpose behind everything is cosmic, spiritual, energetic, theological, or extraterrestrial, we'll never know. But for me, I'd rather live in a world where there is a purpose rather than the absence of one.

I want to leave this place better off than when I found it. I want to leave this world in a better place then when I came into it. So I wasn't a space invader who didn't just go through the motions. I wasn't just an economic contributor. I made this world better. The world was better off because of me. Not in spite of me.

How about you?

That's the business model of life: the lessons, the learnings, the wisdom, the battle scars, the warts and all. That's the meaning of life. That's the message of the last 3+ years. And it's one way to think about the ultimate sacrifice that was paid by so many, through no fault of their own. The ones who didn't make it. Why them? Why not us? We don't know. We'll never know.

FIXING THE BROKEN BUSINESS MODEL OF LIFE

If we want to fix the business model of life, the broken business model of life, it really does come down to one thing, and one thing only. What is that one thing? As Curly said in City Slickers. "That's what you have to discover."

MY PATH. MY WHY

As they say in the world of Instagram or TikTok, I was today years old when I discovered my "why" statement. I needed one that would run through all of my projects like a red thread and in doing so, would allow me to say hell yes or hell no to every project or opportunity that comes my way.

CHAPTER 9 - THE BUSINESS MODEL OF LIFE

This is my Why statement:

As a teacher, facilitator and coach, I help high-aspiring entrepreneurs, business owners and their leadership teams get unstuck, return to growth, and become forever changed.

> As a teacher, facilitator and coach, I help high-aspiring entrepreneurs, business owners and their leadership teams get unstuck, return to growth, and become forever changed.

"See that? [points to a cabin] That's where I was born. Y'Know... one day my... my mother she, put me on her knee and she said to me, 'Gaston, my son... the world is a beautiful place, you must go and eat and love everyone... 'got to make everyone happy, and bring peace and to content with everywhere you go...'. So I became

FOREVER CHANGED

> *a waiter... [grins and starts to slowly stop]... *sigh* well it's- not much of a philosophy- I know but... *sigh*. Well, Fuck you! I can live my life in my own way, if I want too... FUCK OFF! [walks towards his home slowly]... Don't come followin' ME!"*

Thank you Gaston from "Monty Python's Meaning of Life!"

Ultimately my hope and wish is that you will derive your own formula, your own path from this, and celebrate your incredible uniqueness, your magic, your potential, your abilities, your capabilities, your gifts, and your power. Your power to change the world.

Lucky for you, I have a formula which I will share with you shortly.

CHAPTER 10
ERROR AND TRIAL

FROM THOSE HUMBLE BEGINNINGS UNTIL PRESENT DAY (STILL humble), there has been a series of experimentation, trial and error, with both failures and successes. More failures than successes to be fair.

It's all a matter of perspective. As we know, failure is only truly failure when you don't learn from it.

I decided to create a Prime Directive, focused on one goal: audience growth. That remains my Prime Directive to this day, as I envision being acquired by a network like CNBC, Cheddar, or one of the primary streaming platforms like Apple TV, Amazon Prime, Netflix or HBO Max or Max as it is called now.

I won't sugarcoat it; it has been challenging. And it still is. My new tongue-in-cheek positioning: *the best business talk show no one's watching*, or not enough people I should say to be fair. Actually, there will never be enough people as long as there's a single person that is stuck, looking for inspiration, connection and meaning.

Nate Woodbury, a YouTube Producer and past guest on my show told me, "*There are 8 billion people on this planet searching for you. They just don't know who you are yet.*"

Until I crack the code, and I've tried everything, short of going on ABC's The Bachelor - which these days would have to be "The Golden Bachelor" - and besides, I'm also married, in order to boost my Insta followers. Sigh, I guess I'll just keep on trying.

I've tried different times of the day to tap into lunchtime; live and on-demand; even Late Nite Jaffe with adult beverages. I've tried a

FOREVER CHANGED

seated soliloquy (because I'm sitting and it's a monolog) with teleprompters and without, daily correspondents discussing diverse topics like equity, inclusion, cryptocurrency, philosophy, wellness, mental health, and flow, a Creator Corner, where various artists, spoken word poets, musicians, singers, songwriters, TikTok stars, comedians, jugglers, and magicians perform. I tried to secure my version of a Kevin Eubanks or Paul Schaefer—a musical muse, almost like a sidekick. I even had a virtual audience warmer. Who loves ya, Lenwood? I've contemplated a virtual studio audience, using NFT's as a loyalty mechanism to sit front row or come backstage to the green room. Crypto giveaways. Live Tipping.

I'm still trying.

I will never stop, until the day I drop. Dead!

I tried the acronym: WWCD. What Would Carson Do? Johnny Carson. What would he do if he were starting the Tonight Show today? What is Immovable? Open Season? On the table? Fair game?

I wanted to bring entertainment, experience, humanity and authenticity to the world of business and marketing. I still do. Amidst conversations about leadership, superpowers, the new way to work, the great resignation, creativity, collaboration, innovation, and disruption, why not mirror the manic-depressive world we live in with a combination of sublime and ridiculous, as we cover heavy issues interspersed with some REALLY REALLY bad photoshop of my guests' heads on various bodies?

I call that segment Fun Facts.

By the way, fun fact. That segment is now called Two Truths and a Lie, where I come up with a believable fib about my guest, using their bio and background as context.

I've had remarkable guests on the show, including Jamal Mashburn, who discussed his childhood, his relationship with his father, and

CHAPTER 10 - ERROR AND TRIAL

his entrepreneurial dreams. He always envisioned a life after basketball. Patrick Fabian, who played Howard Hamlin on Better Call Saul, who told me his job is to audition; not to act, but to audition. And of course Carole Baskin who volunteered that she did not murder her husband. I never watched Tiger King and now I'm too afraid to tell her that. I've also interviewed Survivor winners, Paralympian bronze medalists, "Cult Escapers" and the list continues.

The vision behind the show has always been focused on HPO: hope, positivity, and optimism, and if there's time left over...a little bit of marketing.

My mother actually started calling it HPO, which lead to my tagline: It's not TV, It's HPO!

I don't want the show to be canned or overproduced. It's just me, myself and I in my home office, with a cheap Wal-mart ring light, a Rodecaster mixing board and my dog barking more often than I would prefer. My canvas is empty. Literally. I have no notes or pre-written questions. Together, my guest and I discuss stories, personal obstacles, adversity, and some life changing insights and lessons. I've disarmed some of the most famous celebrities or poker-faced corporate executives.

At our core, we are all the same—equal in our hopes, fears, and dreams.

> At our core, we are all the same—
> equal in our hopes, fears, and dreams.

In 2020, I reinvented myself. In 2021, I reinvented the talk show. In 2022, I planned to monetize it all. I didn't, but I will.

On December 31, 2020, I created "New Year's Streamin' Eve" as an inspiration to New Year's Rockin' Eve, pioneered by the late Dick Clark. I even used a real company as a fake sponsor. Planet Fitness was the actual sponsor of New Year's Eve in Times Square. Unfortunately, due to COVID, that New Year's Eve celebration was a non-starter, without a crowd in Times Square to leverage their sponsorship. So I reached out to Planet Fitness, but corporate bureaucracy prevented us from striking a deal. They did send me two of their ridiculous Mad Hatter hats. I had a fantastic time hosting the show. Viewers could call in and past guests made appearances. Frank Perrouna Jr., the artist who created the show's theme song performed. It was a two-hour proof-of-concept stream that I thought worked exceptionally well. And to top it off, I got to kiss my wife when the ball dropped at midnight.

This was all part of a grander idea—an idea that aimed to reimagine work-life in a hybrid and virtual existence. Even if people returned 100% to their traditional work routines after the pandemic, there are still plenty of opportunities for virtual connection. The concept still works.

So, I proposed the idea: What if your next status meeting, offsite, workshop, or training course was a show? What if your all-hands meetings or employee onboarding were transformed into a show?

Instead of a meeting...a show

Instead of speakers...guests

Instead of slide decks...overlays and banners

Instead of an emcee...a host

Instead of Q&A....live comments

I received some interest. A construction company called Skyline, General Mills, and almost 10 episodes working with HP. I used this format to deliver an end of year holiday show with prize drawings, award winners announced by the legendary Michael Buffer, raffles, and even an ugly sweater competition. I announced an acquisition and introduced the leadership team of the new company to the parent and subsidiary companies. I even presented the transition of new CEO and quarterly earnings—all delivered exquisitely as a show.

The model worked brilliantly because, as Walt Disney once said, "If you can dream it, you can do it." One person in a home office can power an entire show for a global company.

What a thought.

At one point, I believed this would become my main revenue stream, my day job. I even envisioned an entire network of hosts and shows, where companies could choose their emcee or DJ, just like they would for a wedding or bar mitzvah. I've since moved on from that idea, but if you find it compelling, please steal it—I genuinely believe it has the potential to impact and engage employees who are tired, disconnected, and yearning for something different.

The same concept applies as my morning audio-first virtual coffees.

Steal at will.

STUCK IN MY BUBBLE

It has not been smooth sailing. I've faced numerous challenges with platforms like Facebook (Meta), YouTube, Twitter (X), and LinkedIn limiting my reach. It has been super frustrating trying to break out of my own social media bubble. I have substantial numbers of followers and connections, but it often feels like I'm starting out for the first time.

In the Web 2.0 era, you have to pay to play. Fortune does not favor the bold, but rather the rich. The megabrands. The established celebrities have a seemingly unassailable lead. This is the Matthew Effect and it sucks.

FOREVER CHANGED

Take Jim Halpert in the Office AKA John Krasinski, who created a YouTube show during the Pandemic to focus entirely on positive and inspiring stories. It was called "Some Good News" and after garnering over 71 million views and 2.57 million subscribers on YouTube in just 2 months, he sold it to CBS. And then he just stopped.

"So he made 8 YouTube videos comprised largely of unpaid contributions from fans, sold the brand to a major conglomerate, and isn't even going to make it anymore? Just cashed out? Does this rub anyone else the wrong way, kinda?" <u>tweeted</u> @Lons.

Hey Jack Ryan, I'm still standing. Outlasted. Outplayed, and Outwitted CNN+. I'm still standing. Or sitting.

I've realized I need to shift my focus from quantity to quality, homing in on the power of one. I believe that all I need is one person to watch, stumble upon, or discover the show. That one person also needs to run a studio or network. And if not them, someone who knows them. Someone separated by 6 degrees of Kevin Bacon. Or Kevin Bacon himself. That's the person I'm looking for—a professional soulmate who sees the potential, the freshness, the originality I bring to the table.

I'm still in the game, which means I haven't lost. I once asked a guest, *"how do you know when its over?"* Their response: *"it's only over **when you say it is**."* Or to quote Yogi Berra, "it ain't over till it's over."

It only ends when you say it ends.

It only ends when you say it ends.

The mainstream talk show genre has since shifted towards byte size highlight clips watched after the fact and on-demand, but I continue to believe in the power of live long-form conversations that aren't

CHAPTER 10 - ERROR AND TRIAL

crammed between advertising pods. My inspirations remain Howard Stern, Tim Ferriss, Steven Bartlett...and of course Jon Stewart.

I'm still here, plodding with purpose.

And I won't quit.

I will continue to pour my heart and soul into creating the best talk show on business (and perhaps the only talk show on business), even if it feels like no one is watching, because sometimes they aren't. Each time one of my guests tell me, "I had so much fun" or that this was one of – if not - THE best interview they've ever been on, it refuels and reenergizes me.

I love what I do.

I am being true to myself.

I will stay the course.

Hey, that sounds like a formula...

CHAPTER 11
GROUNDHOG DAY IN THE METAVERSE

There's no bigger sign than the global pandemic, but were we paying attention? Sometimes the signs are there, but we don't see them. Sometimes we see them but choose to ignore them. Sometimes we pretend they're not there until they slap us across the face again and again and again and again. And it's not just the Global Pandemic. It's Olivia Newton John. It's war in Ukraine. It's Jimmy Buffet.

How many times are you just going to get kicked while you're down? At some point, you've got to get up and say, "You know what, I'm going to kick you back."

EARLY WARNING SIGNS

The signs are all around us, but so too are the warning signs. Your tingly *spidey sense*. Your gut. Your intuition.

Not just warning signs, but early warning signs.

"I knew the writing was on the wall when I realized I wasn't growing" said one member of my community to me. And so when they were laid off, it really wasn't much of a surprise. And yet they stayed until they were handed that pink slip. Why?

A CLEAN START EVERY DAY

The daily grind should be replaced with the daily grow. If your time at work is characterized by the former, you are on borrowed time; if your time at work is heralded with the latter, you create a contagious energy which brings with it - longevity. On your terms.

CHAPTER 11 - GROUNDHOG DAY IN THE METAVERSE

Throughout this book I challenge you to live every single day like it is your only day, like it is your last day. Like it is your best day. I hadn't quite thought about the idea of starting from scratch, a clean start—blue ocean, blank canvas, clean slate. Mulligan. What if you could do that every single day? What if you could literally start again every single day? Live every day like it was your FIRST day?

And the reality is, we do—we actually do. We wake up every morning. And some of us, depending on our religion, begin the day by actually thanking God for returning life to us. There are people who believe that when we go to sleep, we essentially die. Our soul leaves our body and goes to some ethereal place. And in the morning, it is returned to us.

Wait, is **that** the Metaverse?

In my religion, we wake up and wash our hands because we're actually washing the death off our hands. At night, our soul leaves through our fingertips and returns in the morning. We give thanks to a higher power for the gift of another day; another chance.

Another chance to write the wrongs. Another chance to correct our mistakes. Another chance to turn good into great.

Or we could squander the chance we were just given by going through the motions. Rinse and repeat. Groundhog Day. SSDD: Same Shit Different Day. What a waste. What a tragedy. Groundhog Day in the Metaverse means we're not growing.

And we should be. Each and every single day.

EMBRACING GROWTH

Many of us start the morning by going to ~~Twitter Blue Sky Mastadon Threads~~ X and say "gm," or good morning. In a way, we're basically saying, *"Hey, everyone, I'm still alive. Made it through the night. I showed up today. I wonder what possibilities are in store for me?"*

Starting from scratch. A clean start.

Today we're going to grow.

Today we're going to make a difference.

Today we're going to change.

Today, we're going to change the world.

DEAR DIARY

Wait you're not done.

You made it through the day, but before you head back to the netherworld, it's time to journal.

Dear Diary,

Today I made a mistake and here's what I learnt from it. Something different happened to me today, and here's how I was able to make sense of it all and become smarter.

Growth implies learning. It implies evolution—getting wiser. It implies movement, moving forward, momentum, elevation, all of the above. Flow. And it implies we didn't waste this one extra day, filled with countless and wonderous chances to move the chains, as they say in American football.

It's in part why Elon and company wrote their open letter, warning the world about the dangers of AI and how and why the world needed **to slow down**. It's the LEARNING part. The AI learns. It learns from its mistakes. It gets smarter. It does not make the same mistake again.

And you guessed it, that's where we fall down, because we don't learn. We never learn. It will be our undoing.

CHAPTER 11 - GROUNDHOG DAY IN THE METAVERSE

Sam Harris recently blew my mind when he drew the following comparison: Let's say the AI machine is exactly as smart as the human – no more and no less. The only difference is the processing speed which is roughly 1,000,000:1. What does this mean? If the AI was a work colleague or competitor, they would process what you could in 20,000 years in just 2 weeks. Let that sink in. I don't know about you, but that's not competitive *advantage. It's Competitive Game. Set. Match.*

IF IT AIN'T BROKE, BREAK IT

I wrote about embracing your heresy in Built to Suck. Are you prepared to put yourself out of business? What if you fired yourself? What if you gave away your product for free and still no one wanted it? What if you slaughtered the cash cow? What if you left money on the table? What if you funded your competitor? By the way, all of these have happened, from REI closing on Black Friday to the late Andy Grove firing himself at Intel, Netflix killing the DVD business and moving completely to streaming.

What if you could start anew every single day?

The concept of a daily clean slate is one of these heresies. What if we could blow the whole damn thing up and start again from scratch? Every single day.

CTR. ALT. DEL.

It's painful. It's cathartic. It's the ultimate rush. It's a game-changer.

Truthfully, it's not difficult to disrupt any business on this planet, any business model or industry. How? Start from scratch. But what does that mean? It means no baggage, no legacy. No incumbent thinking, no politics, no preconceived notions like *"this is the way we've always done it in the past."*

DISRUPTING THE NORM

FOREVER CHANGED

This is why JetBlue was able to disrupt the airline business because they didn't have to conform to the rules of the industry. They weren't tied into long-term contracts and union deals. They were installing live TV and free wifi.

Bonus: Blue Terra Chips.

Which airline would you choose?

If you had to reimagine your industry from scratch today, what would you do? How would you do it differently? What about the education system? What about government? What about the publishing industry? What about YOU?!!!

Don't like the current system? Build a better one. Build a better mousetrap.

SLOW STARTS AND CLEAN SLATES

Here's another thought: when times are tough; when things are slow; when you have more time on your hands, congratulations, you have a clean slate.

> It's not a stay of execution, it's a play of execution

Every slow start offers you a clean start. Every slow start allows you to start from scratch. **It's not a stay of execution, it's a play of execution**—a gift you'll never get again, a little bit more time (as long as you have the runway, of course).

The only problem is that there's never a good time to start again. There's never a slow time to consider starting again. There are always fires to put out. Always distractions. Now if only we had a slowdown or a pause for like, let's say….2-3 years, what might we achieve?

CHAPTER 11 - GROUNDHOG DAY IN THE METAVERSE

PERMISSION TO GOOF OFF
Chill FFS.

If this all feels a little too intense for you, that's totally fine as well. Take a break. Relax. Meditate. Manifest. Take a clarity break. Give yourself grace. Congratulate yourself on making it this far. Take pause. Reflect and journal. To quote one of my guests, *"in a season of learning, growth includes regular rest."*

Perhaps constant activity isn't always the answer.

Just ask your muscles.

We work out. We tear them down, and then they build back stronger, but the only way they build back stronger is when we rest them.

So resting is actually part of growth.

The downtime is when we tend to be inspired, where ideas are born, when we're not being bombarded with all these stimuli and distraction.

Almost every religion has this built into their model.

Divine.

The downtime also gives us pause to take stock.

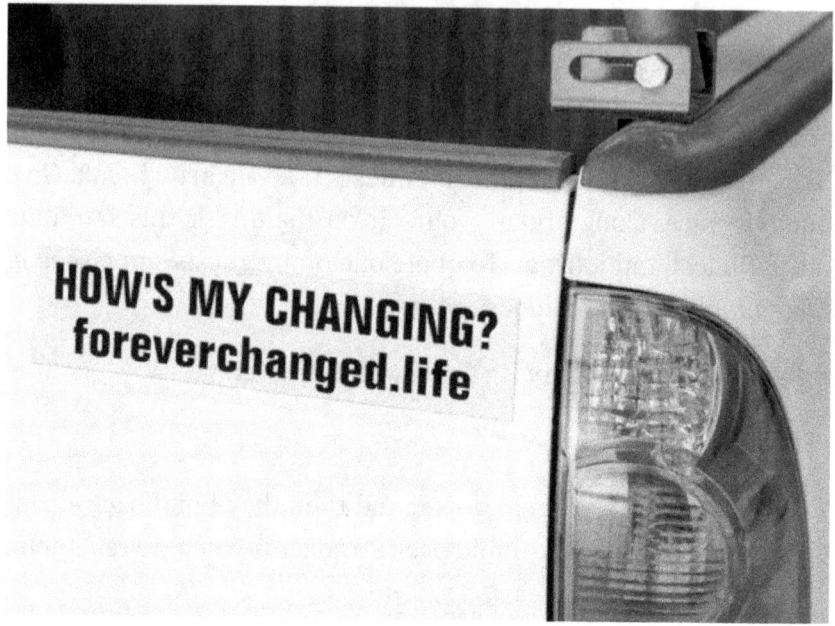

Rome wasn't built in a day, and neither will your transformation.

In addition, you'll need periodic "change-ins" (like weigh-ins but less embarrassing).

How am I doing? Am I on track? Am I ahead? Am I behind? It always helps when you know where you're going, right? Having a destination is integral in order to build a map. Having a goal is integral in order to build an action plan. Sometimes, however, we will need to fly blind and trust the process, trust our gut, trust ourselves.

In either scenario, there does need to be an assessment of whether we've lost our way—or the corollary, which is to discover a better way, an entirely new way.

It could be a shortcut. Or it could be a "longcut." GPS systems will give you options of fastest time, shortest distance, or the scenic route.

CHAPTER 11 - GROUNDHOG DAY IN THE METAVERSE

COMMENCEMENT SPEECH EXCERPT AT 2023 WASHU GRADUATION BY SAMM KAISER

I decided to talk about everyone's absolute favorite thing. Quantum physics. In the spring of 2022, I enrolled in an upper-level computer science class called Introduction to Quantum computing. My biggest takeaway from this class had nothing to do with computers, and everything to do with me. Consider quantum superposition. This concept explains how if a physical system has multiple possible configurations, then the best way to represent it is with a mathematical combination of all these possibilities. To understand the system, we must allow all the possibilities to exist at once, or else we lose part of the picture. In fact, many contradictory things often must be true at once, or the entire system will collapse.

Consider the contradictory mess that was COVID-19. In this new world. An unjust number of people died, and countless more endured physical and mental health crises. It was a great suffering. At the same time, COVID-19 gave many of us a reason to slow down to reevaluate our lives, to start new ventures and work through bad habits, to live through a significant piece of history and reimagine how we could take the Sour Lemon that life had to offer and turn it into something resembling lemonade.

The activism, the relationships and the wisdom that the pandemic left in its wake are beautiful and inspiring. This is not despite an international tragedy, but because of it. To erase the suffering of the pandemic, or to ignore the positive change brought along because of it, is to lose part of the picture. We need both. We need superposition.

Graduation speeches often have advice. I'm going to share what I wish I knew in eighth grade. Now, as we move into the real world, ready to put our hard work to the test, I implore you, slack off. Sometimes be lazy. Take time to enjoy life for what it is without

> *trying to change it. Because the more we enjoy our world, the harder we will work to save it. Achieving the future we want; a future of climate harmony; of Global Equality; of maximized human joy will be an uphill battle. And the more fun we have blowing off work with our friends, napping in the sunshine and laughing over dinner, the more inspired and energized we will be to fight for justice, for equality, for everyone's right to enjoy life. The more we love the journey, the more quickly we will arrive. So work hard, but take time to enjoy the world you are creating.* **Be lazy to save the world.** *It's a contradiction that we must remember. It's a superposition that we must embrace. So Class of 2023 Go forth and slack off. I promise I'll be doing it with you.*

I couldn't have said it better myself.

When we talk about first mover advantage, we typically associate that with speed. In other words, *fast* mover advantage? What if you could achieve first mover advantage a different way? Like the tortoise in the fabled race between the tortoise and the hare.

Slow and steady wins the race.

Translation: grow every single day. Make progress every single day. Generate energy every single day. Establish momentum every single day. No matter how small or seemingly insignificant. And yes, if you've been paying attention, even the days of mistakes or failures, what appears to be moving backward is actually anything but. It is still progress because there's still movement. It could be the discovery of a new path, and when "zoomed out," it doesn't look like negative progress at all.

The "slow cut" comes built in with more time, and more time translates into more. More stimulus, more inspiration, more opportunities to grow, more opportunities to learn and engage.

CHAPTER 11 - GROUNDHOG DAY IN THE METAVERSE

This is the bridge between past, present, and future. All you have to do is connect the dots and find the meaning. All you have to do is determine if what was true yesterday is still true today.

This is why massive airplanes need to go back regularly for recalibration because if the GPS is off by even a fraction of a degree, a heading that is plugged in to the autopilot over the course of several hours can translate into hundreds of miles of deviation from the intended destination.

A massive gap as opposed to gain.

And that is true in life.

THE JUST NOTICEABLE DIFFERENCE OF LIFE

You don't notice it immediately, but over time, it all adds up until you realize you're back in hell. Or worse, back where you started. March 2020. How did this happen? How did I get here? How did I get so lost? How did I get so wrapped up? How did I get so confused or manipulated or taken advantage of? That's the danger of not seeing the signs immediately, and over time, you become blind and deaf and dumb to the signs and numb to the signs. And then worse, you just choose to ignore them altogether.

This is why *WE* need to disrupt ourselves without – and before - waiting for the next Global Pandemic. We might not get that "lucky" the next time around. And by *WE*, I refer to the Human Race and by Global Pandemic, I could be referring to AI that will be a billion times smarter than us mortals by the time we realize it's too late…

Back to Sam Harris: imagine if we decoded a message from a vastly intelligent alien species that read something to the effect of, "hey lowly, inferior humans, we're coming to your planet en masse in 2042. Get ready. See ya…wouldn't want to be ya."

Remember Chapter 1? Besides striking out, we'd freak out. Big time.

And yet, when it comes to AI, it's crickets. No emotional connection whatsoever.

So goof off and then get back to work, but perhaps this time at a different cadence.

TORTOISE, HARE...MEET PENGUIN

In the Grand Animal Kingdom, a unique race was organized like never before, a dual-domain challenge covering both land and water. The typical competitors were, of course, the swift Hare and the steady Tortoise. But this year brought an unusual participant - the balanced Penguin.

The Hare was all about speed, the Tortoise all about perseverance, but the Penguin was different. On land, she was a determined plodder and, in the water, a measured swimmer - embodying the best of both worlds.

Also in consideration, amongst others, was the Donkey, known for his stubbornness (and thus, never giving up), and the Goldfish, notorious for giving up too soon.

The race started with the Hare zooming away on the land segment. The Tortoise began his slow, deliberate crawl, and the Penguin moved at a pace that was neither a crawl nor a sprint - it was a brisk walk.

When they reached the water, the Hare floundered, while the Tortoise and the Penguin were in their elements. Even though the Penguin could dart through the water with a speed that could rival the Hare's land pace, she opted for a 'slow jog' to maintain her consistency.

From the sidelines, the Donkey, ever the sturdy stalwart, nodded in approval, recognizing the virtues of the Penguin's balanced approach. The Goldfish, however, swam away halfway through the

CHAPTER 11 - GROUNDHOG DAY IN THE METAVERSE

race, forgot why he was there in the first place, and promptly gave up.

In the end, the Penguin was victorious, using her unique combination of slow steady progress on land and consistent pace in the water to beat the other competitors.

It was a testament to her statement, "In patience, we find the brisk walk of progress, not the tortoise's crawl of delay, nor the hare's sprint of haste. And in the balance of these paces, we find the truest pace."

Applause erupted from the crowd. The Tortoise was the first to congratulate the Penguin, acknowledging that her approach of consistent, manageable pacing was superior to his 'slow but steady' strategy. Even the Hare had to acknowledge her prowess, admitting that speed alone was not the answer.

Penguin shared her philosophy, "Patience is not just about waiting, it's also about moving at a consistent, manageable pace. It's about having a clear vision and the will to move forward, regardless of the pace."

The day ended with the animal kingdom gaining a deeper understanding of patience.

And now hopefully you as well.

There's always a better way. There's always a new way. There's always a way. Find it.

INDEPENDENCE DAY IN THE MULTIVERSE

Metaverse. Multiverse. There's even a Fediverse nowadays.

A lot has changed, but here's what hasn't changed. Us. We keep on making the same mistakes over and over again, expecting a different result.

FOREVER CHANGED

We don't seem to learn as a species, but you know who is learning? All the time?

Let's try not to remain on the sidelines until it's too late. Take action. Do it today. Do it now. Start with the one person you should be able to trust the most in the world: yourself.

Keep moving. Never stop. Keep grooving. Never stop having fun. Keep improving. Never stop learning.

This is how you make the transition from SSDD (Same Shit Different Day) to DSDS (Different Shit Different Day).

This is how you move from the Daily Grind to the Daily Grow.

This is how to live awake and alive.

Pragmatically Paranoid.

Expecting the Unexpected without having any clue what might be next. Flesh-eating Crab People living in the Earth? I had that in my 2020 Bingo. Fire Tornados? That actually happened in August of 2022 in Los Angeles.

Anxiety is said to be PTSD of a previous trauma manifesting itself in expected future trauma – which may or may not happen. This is when tapping into our superpower of resilience makes all the difference.

We'll *double cross* that bridge when we come to it and when we do, this too shall pass.

And when you feel weak, and you will, zoom out and reach out.

We're here for you because we are you.

Forward.

CHAPTER 12
TAKE THE OFFER

I ALWAYS SAID IF I STARTED A COMPANY, I WOULD TAKE THE FIRST offer that came my way.

And I did.

I sold my company crayon (and sadly, our crayonville island in the Virtual World of Second Life) to the very first bidder and I built a house with it. I traded in my virtual Penthouse for a real house!

I took the offer and didn't second guess it, but now that you mention it...could the second offer have been bigger? Could the second offer have been better? Sure. But it also could have been worse.

I feel the same way with my show. When you see me on a streaming or cable network one day, you'll know it was the first offer that came my way. Of course, an offer still needs to be the right offer and a fair offer, but assuming both are in place, game on.

Progress above Perfection. Plodding with Purpose

THE POWER OF SUFFICIENCY
Take the bird in the hand versus the two in the bush.

There is precedent. We have seen so many examples of companies that didn't take the offer and later regretted it.

Snapchat turned down $3billion from Facebook. I think they probably felt it was a good decision at the time. Or Clubhouse, the Unofficial App of COVID-19 that caught lightening in a bottle, turned down Twitter, that would later go on to launch a competitive product called Twitter Spaces. Then there's Blockbuster and Netflix, GroupOn and Google and many more.

There are other cases, like Instagram, who took the offer and sold to Facebook for $1 billion. I thought it was the most insane decision. I was thinking that the founders must be doing backflips in the shower at the time. Who in their right mind would pay a billion dollars for a photo-sharing app? Facebook, of course! A desperate move by a desperate company. And then a short while later, Facebook bought WhatsApp for $19 billion.

And I shut my big mouth.

I wonder if the Instagram founders regretted their decision. Taking the bird in the hand. I'd like to believe they did not.

They're going to be ok though.

DEFINING "ENOUGH"

In many respects, I think this comes down to the idea of sufficiency.

How much is enough? Isn't a win, a win? Or do we have to torture ourselves with woulda, coulda, shoulda self-doubt designed to maximize our gains and anxiety?

To use a sporting analogy, why is it important to win the soccer match 9-0 when 1-0 yields the exact same result and points?

In the financial world, this translates into buying low and selling high. If it only were that simple. And I've heard that we never truly sell at the top or peak of the high or buy at the trough or bottom of the low—but it doesn't stop us from trying.

It must be nice to have sold Bitcoin at $69,000 on November 9th, 2021, and rebought just 7 months later at $17,567.45 (June 17th, 2022).

CHAPTER 12 - TAKE THE OFFER

It must NOT be nice to have bought Bitcoin at $69,000 on November 9th, 2021, and sold just 7 months later at $17,567.45 (June 17th, 2022).

It will also have been nice to have bought Bitcoin at $69,000 on November 9th, 2021, and sold on April 1st, 2025, when it hit a whopping $321,055. While hypothetical April Fool's date is intentional, as are the forecasts, you are going to think I'm a time traveler if it turns out I'm right. Disclaimer, I get my tips from a giant carrot (follow @therationalroot on X for more)

FINDING YOUR RANGE

When considering an offer, it helps to go into any venture or adventure with a plan, and by plan, I mean a very clear and tangible level (or range) at which you will buy or sell. Most trading platforms have triggers built-in. By automating, you are also self-regulating. So self-regulate yourself when applying for a job, haggling with a salesperson or even discussing a pre-nup!

To this day, I walk into a casino with $200. If I double my money, I leave immediately. If I lose my money, I leave immediately. No rebuys allowed.

The key is to take both the heart and the brain out of the equation.

So how does this work in real life? It works by having a frame of reference, an acceptable range... AND THEN STICKING TO IT.

The more ambiguity, the more FUD (Fear, Uncertainty, Doubt)

Just a little more. One more hand. One more month. One final try. I'm so close.

These are not words of a winner. These are words of an addict.

Whenever entering any kind of relationship, negotiation, or collaboration, it's critical to know your limits (and limitations), which itself is a product of risk tolerance, confidence, and most importantly, budget. On the softer side, being clear about what is enough for you, what is going to give you fulfillment and allow you to live an engaged and even meaningful life, is just as important.

AVOIDING GREED AND EXCESS

The bulls and the bears make money, and the pigs get slaughtered.

> The bulls and the bears make money, and the pigs get slaughtered.

People make money in a bull market. People make money in a bear market. The pigs, however, end up on a BLT at the restaurant we opened earlier in the book.

Knowing exactly what you would settle for—good, bad, or ugly—is liberation. It's not settling at all in fact. At worst, you get to lick your wounds, you lose the battle but still have a chance to win the war; you live to fight another day.

At best, taking the offer allows you to move forward with a full heart, zero baggage and nothing but possibility ahead. You also now have liquidity that may allow you to buy or invest in another project; another opportunity that arguably could be "the one" you were searching for all your life.

Doubt and self-doubt will eat away at you from the inside out and before you know it, you will be rotting and rotten from the core.

A big part of this as well is adopting an abundance mindset, as opposed to a limiting or scarcity one. Although in this case, I would channel or focus this thinking in terms of what you gained versus what you did not; how you benefited as opposed to what you missed out on.

CHAPTER 12 - TAKE THE OFFER

It's like buying a string of tickets to rides at an amusement park and feeling this insatiable desire to get your money's worth by not leaving until all your tickets have been used. Instead of storing the positive memory of the 5 rides you *did* take, you now have the negative memory of the 6th and final ride and the dry-cleaning bill to clean the vomit off your clothes and those around you.

Was it worth it? In this case probably as it makes for a great story, but generally, the opportunity cost is not an opportunity lost but rather an opportunity gained.

One door closes. Another one opens.

Lose the battle. Win the war.

FINDING BALANCE

Money is the root of all evil.

University of Denver research from 2019 identified financial problems as the 5th biggest cause of divorce at 36.1%.

Too much or too little.

Might I suggest the Goldilocks approach to "Take the offer?" Just figure out your "just right" range and recognize that it is different for each and every one of us.

Escape the trap of living a comparative life.

While the only person you should ever compare yourself to is yourself, recognize that even that is problematic insofar that you have a former self, a future self, a younger self, and a CHANGED self.

DON'T LET THE OFFER TAKE YOU.

Some offers are real-time. Some are numerous. Some are mundane. Some are low involvement. Others are life-changing.

FOREVER CHANGED

This is the second time since the dawn of digital that amateurs (hello) have deluded themselves into thinking they were day traders, becoming so preoccupied (obsessed?) with short-term gains that they invariably end up with long-term pain.

The first was the dot-com bubble when startups would seemingly go from launch to publicly traded in weeks or months. There was gold in them thar hills, and we were all focusing on the color green. I remember the second the market opened, I would be mesmerized by the flashing "tech stocks." Green good. Red bad. I probably would have done better had I walked into a casino and put it all on black. Red bad. Black good.

The odds are stacked against you in a casino, and they're equally stacked against you day trading or, these days, "flipping NFTs" or looking for the next Bitcoin, often referred to as an Altcoin or Shitcoin. Even Elon got in on the act hyping Doge Coin.

Except $JAFFE coin—my coin. That's different, of course!

When you walk into a casino, you should be expecting to lose. When you attempt to predict the next "Bitcoin" - you should be expecting to lose.

My dot-com portfolio, together with my crypto portfolio and NFT Portfolio is RED. The color of blood. An invariable bloodbath.

This is not to say you or I won't get lucky at some point. A broken clock is right twice a day, after all. It's just that our time and our talents are better put to use elsewhere.

Instead of preoccupying ourselves with the minutia of an offer-based world, it would behoove us to "zoom out" and focus our energy on the bigger picture.

CHAPTER 12 - TAKE THE OFFER

THE PITFALLS OF GREED

A piece of research among indigenous people found a specific tribe in which anyone who took more than they needed was considered to be **mentally unwell**.

Can you imagine that? Equating taking more than you need with mental illness... because you would have to be unwell to put stress and strain on your brothers and sisters. In a zero-sum game, my gain comes at your loss. And even if it doesn't, the excess demand puts strain on the resources of the entire community.

HOARDING BAD. GREED BAD.

Individual greed almost always impacts more than just the selfish one. From a life partner to a family, to a department, to a community, to a tribe, to an entire ecosystem.

However you interpret or internalize this, the basic message is the same: live to fight another day. Learn from your gains AND your losses. Use one opportunity to help you move to a new one. It might be a sideways move. It might even be taking a – temporary - step back. Of course, it might be a giant leap forward as well.

The key is movement and momentum.

BRING IT HOME

What does it mean to take the offer, as it relates to not just my story, but your story - *our* story? How does it relate to the last 3+ years? I believe that the relevance is that we've been given an offer right now. It's an offer to change. It's an offer to move towards a place where we can have fun, do good, and make money. It's a place where we're all moving. Together, we're all moving together because we all came from the same place at the same time. That's how it relates to us this time.

DIVERSE EXPERIENCES AND COMING TOGETHER

We were all in different places in our lives before the world stood still. Some of us have been held back. Some of us have been oppressed, some of us have been repressed, some of us have come from privilege. Some of us landed with our asses in the butter when the pandemic hit perhaps working for a company that manufactured masks or disinfectant. Some of us were first responders putting our lives on the line. Literally. Some of us were driving the Ubers that took those first responders to and from their places of work. Some of us were stuck at home. And some of us were just stuck in general. Now it's time to get unstuck. Now it's time to help one another.

THE BEAUTY OF UNITY

We were all in different places in our lives, but for a moment in time, we were all in the exact same place at the exact same time.

> We were all in different places in our lives, but for a moment in time, we were all in the exact same place at the exact same time.

The beauty of this time and the beauty of this offer is that it is an offer that we can all relate to. It is an offer that we can all empathize with. It is an offer where we can all say we know where you're coming from because *we were there ourselves*. This is an amazing time for us to come together. At a time when we see more partisan infighting and division; more relationships torn apart; more disconnect and disconnection; more isolation and loneliness than ever before, I would argue that in fact, we've never been so connected. We've never had so much in common.

CHAPTER 12 - TAKE THE OFFER

This is the offer. And hopefully, it is a once-in-a-lifetime offer. Because we may never be in this position again. And hopefully, we never are in this kind of crisis again, either.

INDIVIDUAL JOURNEYS

To be sure, there will be other crises in our lives, and we will all go through them individually and asynchronously. In some cases, we may be able to relate; in others, we may not. I'm 52 years old, and I'm an orphan. And I'm going to have to contend and come to terms with that for the rest of my life. And I'll be able to relate in a certain way to people that have lost two parents. And when others lose their second parent, I'll be able to relate to them in a way that someone who has two parents alive simply cannot.

Which is not to say that I can't relate to someone who has both parents alive either. I'd give them this advice if they'll take it: there will never be enough time no matter what you do. So accept that now. And never ever regret how much time you could have spent because it never will be enough.

FINAL OFFER

This is the offer. Will you take it? Will you take the first reasonable offer that comes along?

My offer to you is to join me. My offer to us is to join **us**. My offer to you is to join our community, come and hang out with us every day when we do our virtual coffee. It's a support group; it's therapy. Reach out to me, and I'll do my best to reach back out to you. I may not always be able to do so, but I will try my best because I can relate to you.

I can relate to you, because I was with you in March of 2020 and you were with me. We were all here; we all experienced it together. We should be able to relate to one another, and this becomes the ultimate call to action. Because when you turn a blind eye, when

FOREVER CHANGED

you turn up your nose, when you turn away, you're turning away from a truth—your own truth. You are lying to yourself. You're lying to everyone else. You're in denial and you are rejecting this once in a lifetime offer - the offer to help, the offer to go the extra mile, the offer to go above and beyond, the offer to love your neighbor as you would love yourself, the offer to make a difference, the offer to leave a legacy.

I know you agree with me.

And I know you can do it. And now, so do you.

CHAPTER 13
DOES MONEY BUY HAPPINESS?

THE LEADING QUESTION

DOES MONEY BUY HAPPINESS? IT SEEMS LIKE A LEADING QUEStion. Almost too obvious. Almost too easy.

Like if someone asked you if you would choose to be good or bad? Well, good.

Would you like to live an easy life or a hard life? Easy.

Do you believe in paying it forward and good karma or bad karma? Good Karma!

These are all obvious questions. Common sense if you will, but how many of us have common sense?

Don't answer that.

It's a fairly straightforward question, though with a more complicated answer. We would *think* the answer is no. At least that's the answer we'd give because that's the answer that we feel someone would want to hear. But deep down, if we're being honest with ourselves, I think we believe money *does* buy happiness.

THE PERSPECTIVE OF THE RICH

Rich people would tend to agree, unless they're preachy and lecture us that money is the root of all evil, in which case we might retort, *"That's rich, coming from you (pun intended), with your beautiful homes, huge boat, and private jet. You're saying money doesn't buy happiness, but I would gladly take all of your possessions and wealth, and you'll be just as happy, right?"*

Wrong.

The question is not as simple as it sounds. It's absolutely not as simple as it sounds.

DISCOVERING THE SWEET SPOT

When you have very little to no money, you are clearly unhappy. And when you have tons of it, there's a degree of unhappiness as well. It's exhausting. Have you ever watched Succession? Turns out the more money we have, the more we desire, and we're never quite happy. Because we're living our lives comparatively.

I imagine a bell-shaped curve or a parabola that perhaps illustrates the relationship between wealth and happiness. Somewhere in the middle, however, is a sweet spot where happiness is maximized, where wealth is sufficient. The Goldilocks effect.

DEFINING "ENOUGH"

Where is that specific moment where you are truly satisfied with your lot in life? How much is enough? How long is a piece of string? Most birthdays, when I'm asked what I want, I say nothing. I really can't say I want or NEED anything, other than the latest Apple Watch when it comes out, but other than that, nothing...

INVESTING IN TRUE RICHES

Of course, there's a big difference between want and need, and it comes back to the business model of life being broken - we live our entire lives, work ourselves to the bone so we can be miserable??? This is why I believe a perfect life well-lived is one in which you expire with $1 to your name; where the real investment was not in stocks, bonds, and crypto, but in fact in relationships... and happiness!

My mom wanted to ride the Orient Express. She wanted to fly first class on Emirates. She didn't. She should have. She worked hard

CHAPTER 13 - DOES MONEY BUY HAPPINESS?

enough. She deserved it. Maybe I'll do that one day in her memory, but I'm not sure it'll have the same impact and besides, she flies first class every day now.

THE LONG-TERM COMMITMENT

Can you invest in happiness? Absolutely and it's a long-term investment at that. It's not a switch. On/Off. It's not binary. I'm happy/I'm sad. It's something that you have to work on all your life. Each and every day. It's a routine.

There is a relationship between money and happiness, but it's a long-term, nurtured commitment and it doesn't follow the norms where more is better; where easy is better.

THE PITFALLS OF WINDFALLS

Easy money often is anything but easy.

Someone won the $1.558 billion Mega Millions jackpot in 2023. It wasn't me. If it was, I don't think I would tell you, but I do think I'd still have written his book.

There's a ton of research, anecdotes, and documentaries that show, for the most part, people who win the lottery end up losing it all. And they're not happy. There's no fun when everyone and their grandmother, long-lost friends, plus your estranged dad come out of the woodwork simultaneously to get a piece of it.

COMPLICATIONS OF A COMPLICATED LIFE

I recently toured a home listed for tens of millions of dollars. The lady of the house had a sit-down closet (which is different from a walk-in closet apparently).

In it were some of the most magnificent formalwear I had ever seen. From the shoes to the hats to the dresses. In fact, there was a replica of the pink dress worn by Marilyn Monroe in the 1953 film Gentlemen Prefer Blondes.

Fun fact: The only pink dress known to survive was auctioned on 11 June 2010 and described as "the most important film costume to ever come to auction." The dress ultimately sold for $370,000.

Come to think of it, it's possible the dress we saw *was* the real one.

Clearly, the owner was "high society" and lived a very active, social, and public life filled with charity events, premieres, and exclusive soirees. And the only word I could think of to describe this life was complicated. It seems like a complicated life. And perhaps exhausting. A life lived for other people. A life where your schedule is not your own. Which is not to say this person isn't, in fact, the happiest person in the world. It's possible they are. Perhaps it's just my emotions talking? Perhaps it's jealousy.

She could very well be the world's kindest, nicest, most generous, and UNCOMPLICATED person who sits on boards of charitable foundations and devotes her life to helping, giving, and contributing, especially to those less fortunate. It's entirely possible that she's the most selfless person in the world.

It must be nice to be her, like it must be nice to have invested in Bitcoin when it was $30 or it must be nice to have sold your company.

Let's reframe that. Yes, it must be nice, but then what?

UNRAVELING COMPLEXITY

There's another interesting relationship worth sharing – the one between age and happiness.

This time it's represented by an inverse parabola.

When we're young, everything is awesome (cue the song from the Lego Movie). We might not realize it at the time, but really, life is

CHAPTER 13 - DOES MONEY BUY HAPPINESS?

good. Sleep late. Groan about homework. Stress out about which of the 10,000 selfies you just took makes it to Insta. The struggle is real.

As we get older, our life becomes more complicated. Why complicated? In one word: money. Education, a mortgage or two, car leases, credit card overdraft. The struggle is REALLY real. I encounter that struggle every single day.

It's significantly harder to quit your day job and have your Jerry Maguire moment (use your inside voice please to show me the money!) Perhaps that's why we loved that movie so much – because we secretly wished that could be us.

There's a reason why they call it a midlife crisis. It's a crisis of confidence. A crisis of the road taken, the one not taken, or perhaps the one we wish we could take…but can't…at least not anymore.

Why not?

The pull of change; the need and want to make the move towards being forever changed doesn't go away; it never does. It's just so much harder when you have baggage; all those loose ends that need to be tied up or untied or tied together or tied in knots.

That is until when there's more salt than pepper on the head of hair (assuming there's hair at all).

The birds fly the coop. The nest is empty. Cue the cruises. No more mid-life crisis; more like a mid-life renaissance which begins at 50, 55 or even 60 these days. Ain't modern medicine grand?

The untethered empty nester is ready to fly (again); to travel; to explore; to discover; to CHANGE. Hang on, I'm not done (and nor are they) – to create, to build, to disrupt, to WORK on their own terms; on their own passions; on their own agenda.

I believe the silver-haired revolutionaries will lead the Community Capitalism revolution. No disrespect to the 20 and 30-somethings, but it's going to be the 50 and 60-somethings who have a pivotal role to play here.

Is this why they call it, "age before beauty?"

PUTTING IT ALL TOGETHER

I sucked at math, but remember I used to get paid by the matrix and so, if I was to represent my assertions visually, it would look something like this.

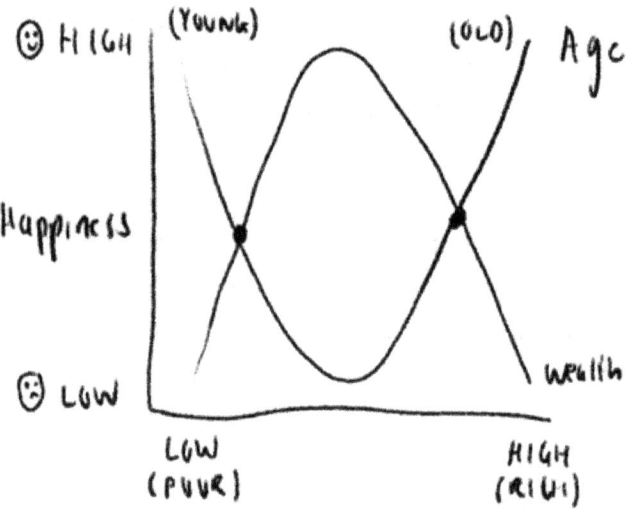

What's interesting to me (and hopefully to you) are the two moments – in life – where the graphs intersect. What are they? Could they be the moments in your life when you are in college and then later, when your last kid has left to college and all of your children are out of the house? Could it be that simple? And if so, does all that college debt count for something? Probably not, but more importantly, what could we all be doing to really maximize happiness potential during these two life windows?

PLAYING ROLES AND BREAKING FREE

I play a role. I didn't realize it, but as a parent, I'm playing a role for my children.

Oh, Dad, you wouldn't understand.

Dad, stay off TikTok.

Dad, that's so cringe.

Dad, you can't do that.

Dad, you can't say that!

Sure, I can! Why can't I? You know I wrote the book on some of this stuff years ago, before you were even born?

We're all playing roles. In your family. At your work. In your communities. You've either been asked or told, or you've chosen to play a role. Speak up. Talk more. Talk less. Stop interrupting. Why didn't you say anything? So typical. I knew you were going to say that.

WE'RE ALL PLAYING ROLES.

Take reality TV, which is anything but real. Most people know this, but a lot of people don't. There's a reason why the participants are called cast members. Why there are auditions. The main characters are really the producers, directors, crew, and cast. In that order. People get recruited, type casted and hired based on filling stereotypical roles. The Cougar. The Psycho. The Villain. The Innocent. It's all *scripted*, not literally with cue cards, but certainly in terms of following a series of narratives and roles.

Jungian archetypes help explain almost every fictional scenario, but equally and increasingly so, in the so-called non-fictional or "REAL" world.

And so we are expected to play our role. You can't act like that. You've aged out. You're too young. You're too rich. You're too poor.

I think we need to break out of these conformist roles, because we all have a unique, original and unfettered role to play. Our own.

ROLES AND HOLES

Instead of conforming to others' expectations, start creating your own. Your age, financial situation, social status, and societal pressures determine the size and shape of the hole you're expected to fit and match neatly.

And what if you don't? How many of you have felt like that square peg trying to fit into a round hole as articulated so beautifully by Apple in their iconic Think Different manifesto.

It's a little trickier in terms of what you do about it.

Do you contour, compromise and customize yourself to become a circle and fit in the round hole? Or do you smash right through that round hole and turn it into a square?

Or do you find an entirely new game to play? Building blocks. Jenga. Whatever.

If the rules of the game are flawed; if the odds are stacked against you, you can try and win the game by attempting to beat "them" at their own game; Respect the rules - after all, everyone's playing by the same flawed rules. That generally means you have to buy in to give yourself that chance – no matter how small. As the saying goes, 99% of short putts never go in the hole.

CHAPTER 13 - DOES MONEY BUY HAPPINESS?

You can also break the rules and live up to archetype of the rebel. Just don't break the law please.

I like the idea of starting a new game. Your own game. Make your own rules. New rules.

Dave Rendall was a past guest on my show. He wrote a book called, "The Freak Factor." He brands himself as the Giant Freak in Pink. One of my requests on my 50th birthday was for my entire family to sit down and watch his appearance on my show. Here's why:

> *I was always in trouble in school and at home, and then eventually at work, because I couldn't sit still, be quiet and do what I was told.*
>
> *Dave, you're never going to amount to anything, if you can't learn to sit still, be quiet and do what you're told.*
>
> *That's the framework that most of us bring to self-improvement. In fact, almost every self-improvement book is, you probably have this wrong with you, or let me show you how you're doing this wrong or not doing this right or failing in this way. And then let me show you how to fix it. And so for me, it was sitting still, being quiet and doing what I was told. And everyone told me that I had to fix those if I was going to be successful. And I wasn't one of those people who was like, I'm going to show you, I'll do it my way. I figured they were right. It was kind of just demoralizing, like, well, I guess, you know, it sucks that I'm going to be a failure. But I don't really know what to do when I'm trying to do it your way. It's not working, you know.*
>
> *So I figured they were right. And then I got surprised. I became an adult, I stumbled into professional speaking; didn't even know it was a thing. And now I get paid to stand up, not to sit down. I get paid to talk, not to be quiet. And I get paid to run my own business, not to do what other people tell me to do.*

FOREVER CHANGED

> *I remember I was sitting in a carwash listening to a book about focusing on your strengths instead of your weaknesses. And I thought, wait a second, what if the weakness is the strength? What if the worst thing about you is the best thing about you? And then they started finding these amazing examples of people all over the world, I mean, dyslexic billionaires and, and there's a guy that I got to speak with who has no arms, and he's the best archer in the entire world, because he doesn't have arms. And because he uses his legs instead. And that gives him an advantage. So I started finding these amazing examples of how weakness was strength.*

New rules to a new game. Your game. The Game of Life. The *Game of YOUR Life*.

Games are fun. Why shouldn't life be fun as well?

"I can't imagine a person becoming a success who doesn't give this game of life everything he's got." – Walter Cronkite

FLIP THE PARABOLA

What if we flip the question and ask, "does happiness buy money?"

This is actually the question being answered in the book.

As it is written in "Do What You Love and The Rest Will Follow," do what you love and the rest will follow!

As we move from the hedonic to the engaged to the meaningful to the actualized life, happiness becomes the supreme currency that can be traded, bartered or exchanged for something everybody WANTS, but not necessarily NEEDS…money.

Whether money buys happiness or not, you had better be happy when you're making that money – no matter how much or how little - or you won't enjoy saving it, spending it, or passing it down to your beneficiaries after the curtain comes down on you.

CHAPTER 13 - DOES MONEY BUY HAPPINESS?

Oh, and I forgot to mention what everyone does immediately after winning the lottery – they go to Disneyland, the happiest place on Earth. Except for the long lines, excess humidity, screaming children, overpriced concessions, and don't forget the gift store!

Don't worry, all your photos that end up on Instagram will be perfect!

CHAPTER 14
ALL IN

I RECOGNIZE I'M A LITTLE BIT OF A MAD SCIENTIST. I WAS INTERviewed in 2022 for an article titled, "The Second Coming of Joe Jaffe" that was reporting on the launch of my premium community, Alpha Collective, which I describe as YPO meets the Illuminati, focusing on Web3, AI, and whatever comes next.

I told Mediapost's Joe Mandese that I felt everything in my life had been leading up to **this**. Everything was converging on this moment.

His dry and snarky response, *"That's what you said last time."*

Is this the boy who cried wolf? Do I lose my credibility every time I dilute the moment with a grandiose statement of intent?

How do you reconcile or come to terms with someone who goes through their entire life saying everything has led up to *this* moment in time…time and time and time again?

Very easily.

It's the same reason why I tell every guest on my show that this has been the best episode and they have been the best guest.

It's 100% accurate.

Until the next show and the next guest and the guest after that.

Every show, I'm getting better, smarter, more evolved. More resilient. Even the shows I mess up. Even the shows with massive technical problems. It's all part of the process. It's all part of the journey.

CHAPTER 14 - ALL IN

It's an empowering thought that reflects we haven't peaked yet. It shows that we're still trying to figure it out until we eventually crack the code.

Some people peak early and make it big really young in their lives. That's okay, too. What you don't want to do is peak too soon and the only way to avoid that from happening is to recognize that everything you have done has been leading up to *this* moment….and then keep growing.

Everything I have been doing has been leading up to this moment. Nothing I do today is the same as before the pandemic.

And I'm going to fight to stay here and not get dissuaded, distracted, disillusioned, diluted, or doubt this path. I won't fall back or step aside, falter, and lose all this momentum and lose this once-in-a-lifetime…gift.

LIFE AFTER THE 30-SECOND SPOT

When I wrote "Life after the 30-second spot," the subtitle was "Energize your brand with a bold mix of alternatives to traditional advertising."

At the time, traditional advertising referred to the big three: television, radio, and print—red, yellow, blue, the three primary colors. My argument was that today, Crayola has their 96-color big box, so why would we choose to create using the same three colors? They might be the primary colors and arguably the three most important colors, but there's more to life. Hence, "life after."

That's why I founded and named a company called crayon.

But life isn't primary.

Life is about the 256 Shades of Grey. Or as *crayonista* CC Chapman described it, "managing the grey" becomes our life's mission and work.

FOREVER CHANGED

The nuance. The subtlety. The originality. The miracle.

Some of the ten approaches in the book may not seem that revolutionary to you today, but cast your mind back to 2004/2005.

Digital. Search. Gaming. Long-form content. Music, Mobile. Consumer-generated content. Communal marketing—defined as marketing to and through communities.

Let's grade these predictions:

Digital: Outspends TV today.

Search: Google's going to make it.

Gaming: There was no Fortnite, Discord or Xbox back then.

Long-form content: No Dollar Shave Club or Direct-to-Consumer brands.

Music: No Spotify.

Mobile: The iPhone had not been introduced.

Consumer-generated content: YouTube had not been founded.

Communal marketing: The term social media had not mainstreamed. Facebook has just been created as a dating site.

Welcome to my life. The pioneer. Always ahead of his time and always missing out.

"There are two types of people in this world: pioneers and settlers. The pioneers get shot and the settlers take the land."

No more.

Right here and right now, I am awake. I am alive. I am full of life. And I am in the epicenter of this incredible Web3 evolution and revolution: shared values, shared ownership and shared reward —a new way to rethink purpose, diversity & inclusion, loyalty and advocacy. It's gorgeous, and it will change everything. It has changed me. Instead of teaching and writing a course or even writing a book about it, I'm actually living it and doing something about it. And no matter what happens, I will stay the course because I love what I do and my life has meaning.

So, who is Joseph Jaffe today?

Joseph Jaffe is a teacher.

I love to help people. I just love helping people. I love it when people come up to me and tell me how I changed their life, their path, their purpose, their trajectory. People who ended up pursuing an entirely different career because of something I said or wrote or tweeted or a keynote I gave. That's what motivates me. It's never been about fame, fortune, or status. It's been about leaving my mark, changing our business, our industry, our lives for the better.

Anything that feeds that purpose feeds my life source. And anything that doesn't snuffs it out. In life, you shouldn't limp in, dip your toe in the water, or test 'n learn. Paying lip service or looking at something superficially doesn't cut it anymore. But taking small steps every day, doing one thing more than the day before, that's how we train for a marathon. That's how we lose weight.

How do you eat an elephant? One bite at a time.

How do you eat an elephant? One bite at a time.

Please don't go and eat any elephants. Get a Beyond Burger instead.

Small steps. Plodding with purpose. Brisk walks. Slow runs. All part of a process that determines when bigger and bolder steps need to be taken...when you go all in.

FOREVER CHANGED

Remember that one small step for you could end up being one giant leap for mankind, but for me, I needed to go ALL-IN on ME. Not just Web3, but Web.Me!

I needed to back myself before other people would back me. I needed to change the way I did business, went to market, and worked. Forever.

I no longer offer any form of consulting. I will no longer be a slave to RFPs (Request for Proposals,) cost estimates, or procurement. I no longer troll speaker bureaus or aspire to be inducted into the National Speakers Bureau Hall of Fame, although I do deserve it!

I no longer am available to have my brain picked because that sounds quite painful.

I no longer am available for free lunches or dinners as a means of enticing me to have my brain picked. I mean, look at me, do I look like I need more food?

Which is not to say that my time is not freely available…for free. It's just on my terms now via my show, the Collective Cafe, or my Substack (which at $8 per month may as well be for free.)

UNLOCKING THE MAGICAL BOX

The key to all of this a token – both fungible and non-fungible or to quote Joel Comm when he was on my show:

"The NFT is a key that unlocks a magical box."

And in that magical box is a series of experiences, interactions, connections, opportunities, utility, surprise, and delight. The beautiful thing is that as long as you own that NFT, you hold the key to unlock that magical box. But when you're done, you can sell that NFT—the digital key—and move on.

It's a whole rethink about the way we do business. We don't need money-back guarantees anymore. We don't need refunds and return policies because everything operates via a secondary market. It's a glorious new way to do business, knowing that there is always a buyer out there. If you bought something, then surely somebody else would buy it too? The law of averages states that there has to be at least one other person in this world (surely more) who feels the same way you do, who is motivated the way you were and would make the purchase for even more money than you paid, based on their perception of value and how badly they want it. This is how all of business is moving.

So I had a crazy idea. What if I could turn my entire community - all of my superfans, past and current clients, viewers, listeners, members of the collective, readers of this book, into salespeople, agents, bookers, managers, influencers and ambassadors? What would happen if I had an army of people representing me? Or moreover, what if WE had an army of people representing US?

The recognition that my assets—my speaking, my time, my brain, my creativity —could all be focused, harnessed, and integrated into the very walking of my talk to demonstrate proof of concept in action. In a world of scarcity and limiting mindsets, why not create a world of abundance?

LESSON LEARNT: BEING ALL-IN VERSUS GOING ALL-IN

If I had published this book a year ago, this chapter would look a lot different. I was contemplating only getting paid in crypto or Web3 currency. No more cash, credit cards or "FIAT" (which is what you normies refer to as money.) I would have looked like a bit of a dumbass. I would be eating digital bananas from JPG's of Bored Apes I right clicked, downloaded and printed from the Internet. Yummy!

I would not be the only one scraping egg of my face. My buddy Justin Bieber bought one of those Bored Ape NFT's for $1.3m in 2022 and one year later, it was worth $60,000.

Does that make him dumb and you smart? Other than his awful moustache, I hazard a guess that his tax write off will not hurt him nearly as much as you or I might feel for denting our bumper in a parking lot or coming back to a parking ticket on our windshield.

Also, we don't know how this story is going to unfold and end, do we? And even if that monkey goes to zero, what did he learn from the process? What did you NOT learn?

Perhaps having this in ink (digital or otherwise) would have focused me even more; to find success no matter what; to find a way to prevail; to find a way to win.

When there's no way back, there is only one way to go...and that is forward.

Maybe I would have gone ALL-IN on going ALL-IN.

Either way, I received the most priceless gift and I'm immensely grateful for it. My gift was the learning that there's a difference between being ALL-IN and going ALL-IN.

There's a difference between being ALL-IN and going ALL-IN.

Going ALL-IN is when you push all of your chips into the pot. It's do or die. It's now or never. If you are the "short stack" (chips, not pancakes; poker chips, not potato chips), you are at your ultimate crossroads, win and you double up; lose and you are out. For some it's calculated and premeditated; for others, it's their last stand; their Hail Mary.

This is not a way to live your life. For some it is. For most it isn't.

CHAPTER 14 - ALL IN

There's a better way. Being all-in means **whatever you do in life. Do it properly. Do it the right way. Put your heart and soul into it.**

100%

THE FINGER

Rex Briggs stood on stage at Microsoft's Strategic Account Summit in Redmond and he pointed his finger stage right. Everyone stared at him. *No, don't look at the finger,* he said. *"Look at where the finger is pointing."*

Web3 is the finger. **Community Capitalism** is where the finger is pointing.

WE > me

Not socialism, but the evolution of Capitalism.

Instead of ESOP's (Employee Share Owned Programs), why not CSOP's (Customer Shared Owned Programs)

I'm just getting started.

How about a book where readers get royalties? Where readers become part of the very ecosystem of the book itself? Built-in influencers, salespeople, referrers.

That's why this book is the world's first book where readers will share in the spoils of the book's success. Shared ownership. Shared reward. 1000 readers become 1000 true fans become 1000 ambassadors become 1000 community members.

Not just a sense of ownership but ownership itself.

> Not just a sense of ownership but ownership itself.

Sharing the love. Sharing the message. Sharing the profits.

Hey, didn't some once write a book called "Flip the Funnel?"

BE THE FINGER

The finger is pointing to the future, but if it's pointing at you, it's a different finger; it's a middle finger and you are its intended target.

This is what it is to be all-in, without necessarily going all in.

I don't need to be a martyr to be a remembered.

I don't need to be a legend to leave a legacy.

I don't need to outrun a cheetah, I just need to be able to outrun you.

Quite frankly the only time I need to go all in is when it comes to life itself and when it comes to life, I'm being and going all in at the same time.

Going all in carries with it the highest risk and the highest return, only in this case, there's a twist. The risk is really an opportunity cost – or rather, the opportunity lost – of not taking your *change* (or chance); shooting your shot; seizing your moment to change forever; to be forever changed. And the return is limitless. The return is your potential realized. The return is your purpose; your passion; your calling.

You can do this. I believe in you. Now **you** need to believe in you.

JOSEPH JAFFE IS A FACILITATOR.

A facilitator is someone who guides a group of people through a process, enabling them to achieve a shared goal. Unlike a teacher, who imparts knowledge, a facilitator focuses on creating an optimal environment for group communication, collaboration, and problem-solving. Their role is less about delivering content and more about steering group dynamics, fostering engagement, and ensuring that each participant's voice is heard. In essence, the facilitator is the enabler of collective intelligence.

Thank you Wikipedia.

Brian Cohen, a bit of a legend in the Angel Investing Community, is an admirer of mine. There's no accounting for bad taste. I forget his exact words, but he once told me – after listening to my show – that I was a translator or something to that effect. An interpreter. He was referring to my ability to connect the dots, frame and reframe, find context and meaning within content; turn conversational straw into motivational gold, through my one-to-one and one-to-many platforms and products.

"There are those who see things and ask why; then there are those who see things that could be and ask why not?" – RFK more recently, but originates back to George Bernard Shaw's play "Back to Methuselah."

JOSEPH JAFFE IS A COACH

It only took me 52 years and one Global Pandemic to complete the series. I've keynoted, taught, lectured, mentored, facilitated, consulted, workshopped, but never coached.

This is new. This is exciting. This is inevitable. This is the most awesome and awe-some responsibility. This is my time.

What a gift, to be able to help business owners get what they want from their business – to run a better business so that they can live a better life. That's the EOS promise by the way, but it may as well have been written for Forever Changed.

During our EOS Focus Day (day 1 of our EOS journey), we kept asking ourselves, "How can we be Joseph's FIRST client?" Sometimes a person is born to do something. That's Joseph Jaffe as an EOS Implementor. If you own or manage a business, and you don't

FOREVER CHANGED

know what EOS is, please reach out to me. You're missing out. So grateful! – Michael LeBlanc, President, CEO & Visionary, CCI Voice

A great coach doesn't come up with the answers because the answers are always in the room. And who's to say, your answer would have been correct anyway.

A great coach understands the power of perspective and zooming out. They are not in the game, they are "on" the game, or rather the sidelines.

A great coach uses and transfers their Sage powers[1] of empathize, explore, innovate, navigate and activate to empower teams to realize their God given potential.

The core values of EOS resonate strongly with me because they embody what it is to be a great coach. Humbly confident. Grow or Die. Help first. Do the right thing. Do what you say.

What are your core values? Do you live them like your life depends on it? Are you all-in on your core values?

As a teacher, facilitator and coach, I help high-aspiring entrepreneurs, business owners and their leadership teams get unstuck, return to growth, and **become forever changed.**

---

[1] Positive Intelligence Quotient or (PQ)

CHAPTER 15
A $PENNY FOR YOUR SOUL

'M ONE OF THE FEW PEOPLE WHO CAN SAY THAT 2021 SUCKED WAY more than 2020. Let's just do a quick recap for those of you that are keeping score.

Was the Insurrection on January 6, 2021 just a friendly "farewell 2020 and don't let the door hit you on the way out" or a hangover and harbinger of worse things to come?

At least for me, it turns out the door was on a hinge, which swung back and knocked the crap out of me.

You already know about the heart thingy, but wait...there's more.

THE CREATOR COIN TEMPTATION

We're going to begin in and around February when a colleague of mine by the name of Jeremiah approached me and asked if I'd be interested in a creator coin.

What's a creator coin?

It's your own branded cryptocurrency.

I was definitely intrigued, but there wasn't a tremendous sense of urgency. I would get to it, in my own time, which was probably never if I know myself. I wasn't enamored with the thought of starting another account on another platform. I can barely remember my passwords on a day-to-day basis, but now I would need to start worrying about something called a seed phrase?

Sidebar: If you've never heard of a seed phrase, you're good, but if you do have one, please send it to me so I can help you optimize your crypto portfolio. That was a test. NEVER EVER EVER send ANYONE your seed phrase. EVER. Not even me!

I'd spent the last two decades building a presence on Facebook and YouTube and LinkedIn, and Twitter and Instagram; a constant, endless and draining battle to get noticed, break through the clutter, defeat the bots in order to be able to engage, attract and hopefully convert into some revenue...and now a new distraction?

You can imagine why I was dragging my feet.

THE FOMO STRIKES

That is until I "saw" or heard (via social audio) the first wave of creator coin launches and their holders talking about their economies.

I want an economy too!

Suddenly the FOMO kicked in. Fear of Missing Out

It was time for me to accelerate the launch of my coin.

You may look towards me today as a crypto enthusiast or Web3 expert, but the truth of the matter is I didn't have a clue in hell what any of this was then, and I probably am in the same boat right now. This space moves super quickly and the only people who say they have all the answers are either liars, fools, scammers or all three.

Sidebar: If you'd like to join my community, just send me your seed phrase. That was a test again. NEVER EVER EVER send ANYONE your seed phrase. EVER. Not even me!

A GLIMPSE OF UNDERSTANDING

I can be a little too self-deprecating at the best of times. Perhaps, I'm being a little too harsh on myself. I <u>had</u> heard of blockchain. It's that building game all the kids are doing online, right? Roblocks? Seriously though, I had consulted on several projects focusing on blockchain pre-Pandemic with my previous company, Evol8tion.

CHAPTER 15 - A $PENNY FOR YOUR SOUL

I had a pretty good idea about the main characteristics and benefits of the blockchain - the public ledger, the immutable nature, and the incorruptible aspect of a decentralized ecosystem.

Now if only I had put my money where my mouth was. I should have bought Bitcoin. I should have bought Bitcoin. I should have bought Bitcoin.

A couple of years ago, my co-founder at Evol8tion, Gina, called me and was filled with anguish. And I asked her what was wrong? And she said to me, "*I can't remember my password to my Bitcoin wallet.*"

I told her I didn't know what she was talking about.

"*Remember back in 2016 when we were in Las Vegas for the Consumer Electronics Show? We met that crazy person who gave us two Bitcoin each? Well, I've lost my password and I can't remember it.*"

Today, I believe we know that password as a seed phrase.

And then she asked me what I did with my coins?

What part of "what are you talking about" did you not understand?

Knowing me, I probably left the thumb drive containing my Bitcoin for housekeeping as a tip. Back then, Bitcoin was probably worth a few hundred bucks. As it turns out, that housekeeper was the founder of Ethereum, Vitalik Buterin. I'm just kidding about the last part, but that story is going to KILL when I do the official keynote.

I should have bought Bitcoin. I should have bought Bitcoin. I should have bought Bitcoin.

So vague understanding of Bitcoin, but no clue about anything else. Ethereum. Is that a gas? I didn't know what the hell an NFT was. I'm not even sure NFT's existed in February of 2021. They probably did, but there were no Bored Apes, No Yacht Clubs and no Bored Apes on Yachts in Yacht Clubs. That came in April.

I hadn't heard of DAO's (Decentralized Autonomous Organizations.) I was starting to hear about this thing called the "Metaverse" and it irritated the hell out of me because I thought they meant Multiverse - and how lame was it that people were trying to reclaim a concept that should have been left to the purity of Marvel comics books. For the record, I still have not set foot in the "Metaverse" mainly because I was in the "Metaverse" 17 years previously with crayon.

SECOND LIFE. THE SECOND COMING OF JOE JAFFE. THE SECOND LIFE OF JOE JAFFE.

crayon never had a physical office; we didn't even have a digital office in the form of a standard website. We had an entire island called *crayonville*. Our website was just a postcard that said "join us **in** crayonville" and when you clicked on it, it opened up Second Life and teleported you to our island.

On our island, we had a movie theater where we once actually premiered a movie that streamed live into our island. And I lived in a beautiful penthouse suite with amazing art. I don't believe they were NFT's. And we had a lookout post where you could watch the sunset and moon rise, and as often as you wanted, you could toggle between sunrise and sunset, full moon, waxing or waning. Very Truman Show-esque. And we had a diner where we would conduct job or press interviews. Such a cool way to rethink talent, and rethink collaboration and connection. And we had a fantastic office. In fact, we would hold our status meetings in a glass conference room, with our PowerPoint status and agenda slides displayed on a large screen. If people were hanging around our office, they could peer in and actually see what was on the slides. We were strategic. And we had pool parties on our roof with live music being performed and streamed in by independent artist, Matthew Ebel through Skype.

CHAPTER 15 - A $PENNY FOR YOUR SOUL

Every Tuesday, we had coffee with crayon, where 30-40 industry folks would meet and talk about marketing, technology, and social media.

REFLECTING ON THE PAST

How interesting is it that 17+ years later we're all talking about the same things. These days, I run a virtual coffee every weekday morning in the Discord server of my project Alpha Collective. We've come full circle. We've come so far and yet we haven't moved at all. In fact, we've lost time. We've lost initiative, we've lost opportunity! We've lost momentum. We've wasted time.

Trusting and putting our faith and stock in lazy journalists, false prophets, scammers, naysayers, critics, and skeptics has talked us out of something that could have been beyond transformational. Where might we be today? Had we not lost interest or faith or trust in Second Life or virtual worlds at the time, what kind of innovation could have been pioneered then, that would be considered commonplace today? And with it, influencing sectors like training, education, people with disabilities (yes quadriplegics can fly in the virtual world), and more.

Please don't give up on your forever changed journey. See the chapter on Stamina.

SEIZING THE OPPORTUNITY

So here we are. Back to the Future. March of 2021 and FOMO gives me the nudge I needed to "just say yes."

Now I will tell you, it's the easiest thing in the world to say no. It's much tougher to get to yes. Just say yes and figure it out later should be all of our mantras. Instead, what we get back from our bosses, investors, clients or even spouses are "my concern is," which to me, is like fingernails on a chalkboard.

FOREVER CHANGED

Why do people immediately focus on the negatives?

It's hard to get to yes. The longer you think about it, and the more time you take, and the harder it becomes.

Just say yes. And then figure it out later. Figure it out later because you will figure it out. You have to figure it out. You always figure it out. Just say yes because "my concern is" is just a slow boat to no. And it will almost inevitably end up at no. This is why, to this day, I would rather get a quick no than a slow yes. Life is too short to draw it out and string people along.

So just say yes or just say no. Both outcomes are probably better, but don't waste your time and don't waste mine.

It's not enough to make decisions. Success lies in making them quickly, changing them slowly, and acting decisively.

> *Napoleon Hill in his book, "Think and Grow Rich" introduces some very interesting insights on procrastination and decision making Successful individuals display a unique decisiveness; they make decisions promptly and steadfastly adhere to them, changing only when necessary and after thoughtful consideration. Conversely, those struggling with wealth accumulation tend to be indecisive, frequently altering their choices and thus missing the boat to success.*
>
> *Interestingly, one's susceptibility to the influence of others also plays a role in financial success or failure. Those who fail to accumulate wealth often yield to external opinions, whereas successful individuals show a balanced approach: they may consider others' opinions, but ultimately make independent decisions about half the time.*
>
> *The decisive differentiator, though, lies in taking prompt action. Procrastination is a silent enemy of success, while the fear of judgment can create crippling inferiority complexes, inhibiting deci-*

CHAPTER 15 - A $PENNY FOR YOUR SOUL

> sive action. Therefore, trust in one's abilities and self-confidence are pivotal.

In fact, making the WRONG decision TOO QUICKLY is better in the long run than making the RIGHT decision TOO SLOWLY – and even better than making no decision at all!

And so I made the wrong decision quickly. I said YES. I launched my own crypto currency, the $JAFFE coin.

ENTERING THE CRYPTO WORLD

In the early days, I actually felt quite insecure and self-conscious about telling people to buy the coin. As I discussed more recently with Dr Francine Hardaway, a fellow coin holder (the $KARMA coin and it turns out it *is* a bitch), there is an early adopter tax or as she put it, "being burnt by early adoption." It's fine I guess when you're the person getting burnt; less so when it's a friend, loved one or perfect stranger.

Sure, this was an absolute pivotal moment in terms of laying the foundation for me to really embrace, lean in, and then go all-in on Web3, but would everyone else see it that way? My holders were beyond supportive and understanding and this was for two reasons:

1. They understood the parameters, risks and nuances
2. They trusted me

They stuck with me through experimentation with my show (from airdrop giveaways to perks like walk on roles for holding a certain amount of the coin.) They essentially got a first row seat in an untried, untested and unproven paradigm of blockchain-backed loyalty, advocacy and community benefits and utility.

Beyond the show, I used my coin to take attendance in my classes at NYU and Western Connecticut State University. Students would use a QR code which was only valid during the hours of class. They'd get a coin dropped in their wallet in return. "Proof of Attendance" worked well because it was "on brand"; I was teaching classes on Brand Strategy, Strategic Communications, International Business, and Principles of Marketing. What better way to teach about innovation than to actually use it?

THE VALUE OF CURRENCY OR THE CURRENCY OF VALUE?

Back in 2010, I kind of predicted the tokenization of loyalty and value when I wrote Flip the Funnel. I called it "universal currency" then, and I made a prediction that every brand would have its own universal currency. Coca Cola would have a $RIBBON (that's the name the company gives to the wave in their logo), Nike would have a $SWOOSH, Target would have a $TARGET, and Starbucks would have a $MERMAID. Or is it $MERPERSON?

Currency can be bought, sold, traded, exchanged, held, gifted, or redeemed. This branded currency would unite, integrate, and unify not just all interactions, transactions, and experiences with customers but indeed with employees as well. One central ecosystem with a direct path to access, assets, and experiences.

Now, I had no idea that corporations would be beaten to the punch by individuals, personal brands, and specifically creators. Also, I had no idea that the actual delivery mechanism or technology that would power this prototype would be the blockchain and specifically cryptocurrency.

WINTER IS COMING

The story sounded great on paper:

Creator Coins, Brand Coins, Company Coins, Country Coins, Sports Team Coins—the list continues—would revolutionize community, advocacy, loyalty, and business as we knew it. I knew it then. I know it now.

CHAPTER 15 - A $PENNY FOR YOUR SOUL

Unfortunately, so did the scammers, "executives" with highly questionable ethics, and the government. Interestingly enough not necessarily mutually exclusive!

Self-interest, special interest, human nature and FOMO are not names of a new punk band.

Cue the great debate as to whether these tokens were regarded as securities. Shocking I know that the SEC and the powers that be might lean towards reinforcing the status quo. Perhaps we should have named this category "Insecurities?"

Despite the fact we were witnessing the spark of a revolution and with it, the first glimpse of "Community Capitalism" in the form of Fractional or Micro-Ownership of not just Corporate Brands, but Human Brands as well, including – but not limited to – Creators, any moves to take away power and control from central authorities and institutions would be regarded as a threat.

"Oh, I get it... this is like investing early in a brand—or band—like stock in humans, right?"

Shhhh, don't say it too loud. You never know who's listening, unless of course it results in more taxes to the government, in which case the response will inevitably become, LOUDER!

There is nothing as powerful as an idea whose time has come. – Victor Hugo

We certainly rode the rollercoaster of irrational exuberance. It was dot com days all over again and the Pets.com sock puppet was (allegedly) deep into planning to come out of retirement in order to release a bright and shiny NFT collection.

WINTER CAME

It's funny, because when things are great, you become complacent and even a little bit greedy. You're on a ride to the moon, so buckle up and enjoy the ride. But when things are bad, you forget the good times, you wallow in self-pity, and can't imagine they'll ever return to "the good old days."

Many of the early adopters got burnt and promptly fled; many gave up; many abandoned ship; many (I call them cockroaches as a term of endearment, because cockroaches are survivors, or perhaps you would prefer rats) moved to the next bright and shiny object, AI or Artificial Intelligence.

The cycle always continues – both in terms of hype and hope.

People have short memories, lack of faith, and ultimately all that is needed is to zoom out to realize it's not really Winter in Game of Thrones at all, but just a little cold snap. So instead of hitting the abort button, why not just bundle up, put some logs on the fire, make yourself a Hot Toddy, and wait it out?

This too shall pass.

THE DEATH AND REBIRTH OF $JAFFE

My Web3 adventure began with a chance direct message that I could have easily just glossed over. Perhaps I should have, although I would not be where I am today.

"*Should happens*" and even though I wonder what would have happened had I ignored the offer to drop a creator coin, living to fight another day is a victory in of itself.

The entire ecosystem collapsed and the "sidechain" (think of it as a branch on a larger blockchain tree) crashed to the earth. 300+ creators and their communities are now completely gone. I however am not. My coin lives (it's hibernating) and is waiting for the next cycle or wave.

CHAPTER 15 - A $PENNY FOR YOUR SOUL

SPRING FOLLOWS WINTER AND SUMMER FOLLOWS SPRING

If luck is what happens when preparation meets opportunity, then catching or riding the next wave or the next groundswell is less an art or a science, and more about two things:

1. Putting in the reps
2. Sticking around long enough

I've been preparing for this my whole life.

Everything has been leading to this.

Now where had I heard that before?

CHAPTER 16
THE FORMULA

I've been hinting at where this book is going for a while now, and it's time to reveal the formula. A formula to embark on this journey to change forever; to be forever changed - a cheat code, if you will, a hack.

What if you didn't need a global pandemic to change? What if you didn't need death or divorce? A tragedy, a major life change, a midlife crisis, or as I've alluded to in this book, a midlife awakening, which, is not age-dependent and besides, 50 is the new 40.

What if there was a formula?

RECOGNIZING THE NARRATIVE

Let's take a step back for a moment and revisit the logic flow of this book, which basically says, if you didn't change during this Global Pandemic, then you missed "an opportunity."

And of course, I take great lengths to always be sensitive to the incredible tragedy and despair of COVID-19. But the fact is sometimes out of crisis, out of despair, out of ruin comes reinvention, rebirth, reinvigoration, and transformation. The phoenix rising from the ashes.

And that is the point. There's always something good that can come out of something bad. The gift.

There's always something good in every human being, even in every bad human being. There are always redeeming qualities. The spark.

There's always truth in any one statement, no matter how much you despise it or the person behind it. Come to think of it, if you get out-

CHAPTER 16 - THE FORMULA

raged or offended or triggered by a statement, it's because there's an element of truth in it. If there wasn't any truth, you wouldn't pay attention, you wouldn't care. You wouldn't feel anything. If anything, you would dismiss it, you would laugh it off, you would minimize it because it has no impact or effect on you, because there is no merit to that statement.

So if it is true that there is truth in everything and everyone and there are redeeming qualities in everything and everyone, then there has to be something good that came out of this Global Pandemic. A sign or signal that perhaps your priorities, my priorities, the world's priorities, humanity's priorities were not aligned; that we were misaligned, that we were off-kilter.

Today we are facing multiple existential crises, from climate change to AI. The open letter on AI has expressed unbelievable concern and reservations about where we're heading in our exuberance, in our race to the bottom. One of the things that I picked up in an interview with Mo Gawdet, one of the architects and pioneers of AI during his time at Google and other institutions, was that the probability of the machines rising up – like Skynet - to *take down* the human race is unlikely. In fact, he gives it a probability of zero. Why? Because before that happens, humans will try to destroy humans using the same tools and technology. And that is the bigger concern; that is the bigger problem; that is the bigger challenge.

HUMAN NATURE

There is another element of human nature and human psychology that is critical here. And it is the fact that if everybody in this world chooses to do good and be good, chooses to abstain, chooses to stay indoors for one week, two weeks, and mask up, then everybody wins. But there's always someone that's going to break the line when we are expected to hold the line, not toe the line, but hold the line... Someone will always break the line. Someone will always take the offer and undercut the competitor.

Self-interest is our Achilles' heel.

The second major statement in this book is that it shouldn't have to take a global pandemic to change forever; to be forever changed... but it helps. The fact remains, we need a push. And oftentimes, it is when we are pushed that we make the change.

MY PERSONAL PUSH

I'd like to take you back to 2002. I was working at TBWA\Chiat\Day, a Madison Avenue agency in New York City. I was running interactive media. I had a small department underneath me. I was on top of the world. I was a father for the first time. I'd been promoted. And I'd started building, unbeknownst to me, my personal brand and my thought leadership platform, writing for various publications, online trades, and magazines. I was invited to all the conferences; I was sitting on all the panels. In hindsight, perhaps I was getting a little too big for my boots while enjoying the limelight. My intent was that if I won, then the agency won because our clients would win. Not everyone saw it that way.

My funny accent, combined with a healthy amount of "Jaffe Juice" (passion, truth, provocation), seemed to work. Everybody loved me. Everybody wanted more, or at least that's what they told me because they wanted my budget. Now, at the same time, there was a global trend happening within the advertising world - the unbundling of media from the advertising agency. Advertising agencies have various departments and functions. There's account management, there is traffic, there is production. There's the creative department. There's the media department. And the current trend was that all media departments were being spun off, unbundled, and then consolidated within holding companies. So the holding company of my agency, Omnicom, was putting together their version of this offer-

CHAPTER 16 - THE FORMULA

ing called OMD and absorbing the media departments of five different agencies: TBWA\Chiat\Day, DDB, Tribal DDB, Rapp Collins, and BBDO. I know, acronym city.

All of my counterparts at the respective agencies took up the initiative and began collaborating. We didn't want Digital to be lost in the shuffle. We even branded our new consolidated department, OMD Digital. Now you understand why the creative people sit in the creative department.

I thought there was a really, really good chance that I was going to run the whole thing. I felt like I was capable, competent, skilled. And of course, I had all of that publicity pixie dust the industry loved so much.

We met every week at a different location. On the fateful day, the meeting was being hosted at my agency. I was literally walking to the meeting when the head of HR (these days "human resources" is anything but human...more like henchman resources; lackeys for the number crunchers and pencil pushers) conveniently popped her head out of the office right as I was walking past and said, *"Hey Joe, do you mind stepping in here for a second?"* I thought nothing of it, sat down, and she parroted the same dead script I had said to some of my own department when I had to let them go a short while back.

"As you know, things have been a little bit challenging... blah blah blah... the economy... blah blah blah... digital... blah blah blah... and yeah, we're gonna have to let you go. Mmmkay?"

I remember my reaction. I actually said to her, **"Are you joking? Is this an April Fool's?"** I was looking around for hidden cameras. There weren't any.

She offered me a paltry two weeks. I had an 11-month-old and was paying rent in a luxury New York high-rise. She shrewdly upped that to three weeks only if I signed a non-disparage agreement.

FOREVER CHANGED

I was shell-shocked. I walked into the CEO's empty office (he would later be "laid off" as well) and called my wife. I remember that feeling, you see it in movies, when the camera suddenly just zooms in and stops one millimeter away from your face. Whooosh. That vacuum, that sucking in.

I remember saying to my wife, *"I've been laid off, but don't worry, everything's going to be okay."*

I'm not sure if she believed the lie. I'm not sure I did either.

During this initial period, I went through the seven stages of grief. I tried to rationalize and understand what had happened... and why it had happened.

Perhaps it had been that I was too resolute, stubborn, and aggressive on my digital evangelizing, even though I was right! See?! *Digital is going to take over the world, level the playing fields, David's going to slay Goliath...* "Digital is the greatest revolution in marketing and media since television."

I would later go on to write "Life after the 30-second spot."

With hindsight, in pushing my agenda so passionately, I'm sure I didn't make friends along the way. Political suicide. Maybe I pissed off one too many people.

In reality, it probably had nothing to do with me at all. It had everything to do with numbers, in particular revenue. If you looked at all the media directors that were coming together, there were about five of us vying for one position, and as it turned out, I represented the lowest revenue contribution. I didn't have a chance. Why would you give the role to someone that represented 8% of revenue when there was someone who represented close to 40%?

The person who got the role was my friend, Sean Finnegan. And he probably deserved it.

CHAPTER 16 - THE FORMULA

He came on my show in February 2021.

In April 2022, he dropped dead.

At the best of times, life appears to make no sense. There is no meaning unless you look for it. And even so, it's hard to assign any value to that meaning.

There I was hurting and wounded, and perhaps bitter and possibly jealous - all these negative emotions. Both happy for my friend and sad for me; angry at the world and perhaps euphoric at the same time for being "liberated."

But if not for all of this, I would not be where I am today. I would not have started keynote speaking. I would not have written six books. I would not have started multiple companies. I would not have become a teacher, an adjunct professor at NYU. I would not have become a talk show host. I would not have become a coach.

None of that would have happened.

Would I have liked to trade places with Sean then? Of course. Would I have liked to trade places with Sean now? Obviously not.

These are not the things that happen to you. These are the things that happen for you.

You may not see it at the time, you may not realize it at the time, you may not appreciate it at the time. But it will be revealed if not in this lifetime, then in the life to come.

Things happen for a reason; we just may not understand it or fully appreciate it.

It took being laid off to force me to make the change. I remember shortly after I hit the ground, an industry friend (and now a personal one) Matt Gilbert reached out to me. Matt headed up sales for the search company, Ask Jeeves.

He was putting together a sales conference out in San Francisco. He asked if I would be one of their guest speakers. I wondered how much I would have to pay to be able to come to this event. Turns out they were going to pay ME - $5,000! I almost fell off my chair! $5,000 for an hour of my time? Turns out they would also cover all of my travel and entertainment costs as well. Business class no less.

The night after I presented, we ended up going to the CEO's house for a cocktail party. Everyone was falling over me as the VIP guest speaker. Everybody wanted to talk to me, including the executives and the board. And I started doing the math. I realized I could earn exactly what I was earning at the agency for only one-third of my time. What would I do with the remaining two-thirds? Double or triple my revenue? Do something else?

THIS was the gift that had been handed to me, untidily wrapped in a personal crisis.

IT SHOULDN'T HAVE TO TAKE A CRISIS TO CHANGE, BUT IT HELPS.

Did you change during the pandemic? Are you changing? How far are you on the continuum from "not changing at all" to becoming forever changed? If you have changed, have you slipped back and reverted to your old self? How do you avoid slipping back and ensuring this transformation is permanent?

What if there was a formula?

Well, there is.

The Formula: Love What You Do, Be True to Yourself, and Stay the Course

CHAPTER 16 - THE FORMULA

The Formula: Love What You Do, Be True to Yourself, and Stay the Course

And if you do these three things, surely only good things will come; only good things will follow, including but not limited to money. Because as we've discussed; as we found out, money may not buy happiness. But happiness buys money or earns money or creates money.

If you love what you do; if you're true to yourself; if you stay the course - if you just hang in long enough, plodding with purpose, combined with continuous change, it's not an "if," it's a WHEN.

THE POWER OF COMMUNITY

The remaining chapters of this book will talk about and focus on this very subject: that we can coach ourselves, we can create change, we can be the change, we don't have to wait to be thrown in the deep end with the bloodthirsty Piranhas; we don't have to wait to be thrown into crises to be plunged into despair, to lose a spouse, to lose a parent, to get divorced, to go through some kind of existential midlife crisis, to be laid off, to experience war, famine, pestilence (feels like we're going through the 10 plagues and we DON'T want to get back to Noah, nor boils, frogs, lice, which is actually describing my kids' last summer camp experience!)

But seriously, this is a process. Life is a process. Life is a project. We have the ability, we have the skills, and guess what? We have each other.

We have this incredible built-in support structure called community.

Today, community exists on multiple planes. There's your family, there's your friend circle. There's your work environment, there's your industry. There's your church, temple, synagogue, mosque. There's your pickleball or Poker group that meets regularly. And then there is socialdipity or metadipity. Your virtual community, whether that is in the metaverse, the multiverse, the fediverse, the omniverse, the herbaverse, it doesn't matter.

The fact is, there are strangers out there that will oftentimes show you more care, love, support, and empathy than people that actually have the audacity to call themselves your friends or even your family.

Don't ask me why this is the case, it just is.

There are perfect strangers out there that can be perfect. Maybe there's something about anonymity that endears people to each other because it's kind of natural to us to want to help, to want to be kind.

I experienced this when I was in the hospital after heart surgery. Strangers popping out of the woodwork with hearts bigger (and healthier) than I could imagine, juxtaposed against familiarity that bred contempt from those who supposedly were part of my support structure.

RANDOM ACTS OF KINDNESS

The highest level of charity is when you give anonymously, and people receive anonymously. You don't know who you gave it to, and they don't know who they received from. That is the highest level of charity because there's no status, nor obligation. There's no awkwardness.

This is what happens when I donate blood as a regular blood donor. 60 units donated lifetime. I don't know who I'm giving it to, and they don't know who they got it from. But I know that I'm potentially saving a life, and they know that somebody volunteered and helped save their life.

The existence of a formula, equation, or recipe is good news for you, and it's good news for me too.

CHAPTER 16 - THE FORMULA

Just like my story, it's my formula. Maybe you will hack this formula. Please do. Please add to it, please subtract from it, please revise and build on it. Please communicate your work and progress back to me. This should be a work in progress, and it should be group work. It should be a collaboration - a team exercise where we continue to build on thinking that can benefit so many more people than just myself or yourself.

Like the series Iron Chef, the theme ingredients are "Love what you do, be true to yourself, and stay the course" but how you customize, interpret, personalize, internalize and implement – aaah, that's where the real magic happens.

Before you get too giddy, I want to emphasize that the road ahead is not going to be plain sailing. There are going to be tough decisions and big realizations that present themselves and manifest along the way, even as a crisis of confidence.

You're going to doubt yourself. A lot. You're going to be scared. Shitless. You are going to anguish on whether you have the strength, courage and ability to make the move; the leap; the commitment to change.

How on earth do you cut the ambilocal chord of safety and security? I can't tell you exactly that, but I will remind you that there will be times when you are pushed, OR you can pull; pull yourself towards yourself...your authentic self. Traction versus Distraction. Pull yourself towards the essence of this formula, which is all about happiness, meaning and purpose. Leaving a legacy.

While we may not understand it or fully grasp it or conceptualize it – now or ever – we hopefully recognize we're part of something so much bigger. We have a role to play. Without us, the world ceases to exist. Without us, there is a hole, a tear in the very fabric and fiber of the universe because... say it with me people: we are miracles.

Now go and change the world.

Get to work.

CHAPTER 17
AMOR

Love what you do, and the rest will follow

THAT QUOTE IS ATTRIBUTED TO MANY PEOPLE INCLUDING Confucius, Marc Anthony (not sure if it's the Roman or Singer), Oprah Winfrey and now myself.

I used to think that "the rest" simply referred to money. At least I did before 2020, but what is the rest? Is it actual rest, as in the ability to enjoy life, avoid waking up in sweats, get to appreciate life, give yourself grace, or the ability achieve a brief moment of clarity? Perhaps it's all of the above, or perhaps it's happiness.

The previous chapters explored the relationship between happiness and money. Now we explore the one between love and happiness.

There's no question that love and happiness are interconnected. If you were miserable before the pandemic, why on earth would you go back to it? Why wouldn't you at least try to rectify it? When you love yourself, you might stand in front of the mirror, not like Icarus falling in love with his own reflection, but actually loving who is staring back at you.

LOVE AND PRIDE

Love's partner here is Pride.

Again not Icarus pride, but more along the lines of *"I'm proud of myself and what I achieved. My mother would be proud of me, my father would be proud of me."*

Where does the money factor into this equation? It doesn't because it never was about the money.

IS LOVE ENOUGH?

when it comes to loving what you do, you can absolutely LOVE harming yourself; harming others or taking advantage of them, exploiting or abusing them (they call these people sadists or politicians) but are they truly happy? Are they being true to themselves?

In a relationship, "I LOVE YOU" are not three magical words. They're just three words that have to be followed up with action—meaningful and consistent action. And sustained action. You must be all-in on love. Love that leads to spreading it.

Want a simple example? Customer service. It's pretty simple to determine whether a telephone agent, cashier or salesperson loves their job or not. The answer is how they invariably end up treating you.

THE DANGER OF INCONSISTENCY

It's the inconsistency that will kill you. In anything—in brands, in relationships. When my friend 4-chair-turn-on-the-Voice Manny Cabo was on my show talking about fans, he told me, *"I can handle the crazies because they're predictable."* It's the unpredictable people that are the most dangerous.

This is why FBI profilers are called "profilers" and why they are great at what they do. Because the people they're ultimately hunting down and catching are predictable. But it's the unpredictable ones that are the hardest to figure out and catch. They're not playing by the rules.

LOVE AND WORK

Same concept should apply to work. Is it good enough to love what you do, one day a week? And the other four to be miserable? Or what about loving what you do for four days a week and hating the fifth? Or one day that's awesome, one day that's awful, and three days that are meh. And worse, not knowing which day is which, especially when influenced by an inconsistent co-worker or unpredictable boss. Call the FBI Profilers!

It makes me start to realize we've made allowances and concessions for far too long. We've excused bad behavior for too long. We haven't stood up for colleagues, for the downtrodden; we haven't stood up to bullies in life, in love, in work, and in play. Abusive bosses, verbally, and unfortunately sometimes abusive parents. We've always made concessions. We've been gaslit and teased with the hope and the fumes that maybe—just maybe—next time will be different.

It won't.

In these toxic relationships, we are fed "just enough" in order for it to be good enough.

Good enough is not good enough.

It's time to be fed....up.

CHAPTER 17 - AMOR

POURING LOVE INTO ABUNDANCE

When it comes to love, there is only one path forward, and that is to pour into abundance. It has to flow and seemingly be never-ending. There should be no limits. The more you love, the more you will be loved. The more you pour in, the more you'll get out.

> This isn't about living to fight another day. This should be about loving to live another day

This isn't about getting by. **This isn't about living to fight another day. This should be about loving to live another day.** Love needs to be channeled, focused, and harnessed to become the ultimate killer app.

I've had so many guests on my show that are masters in love. Tim Sanders who wrote "Love is the Killer App." Moshe Engelberg who wrote "The Amare Effect." There are plenty more like Matt Thieleman who talks about becoming a "Warrior of Love" and guess what, you can be victorious in love in so many ways.

In the book, "The Gap and the Gain," we learn about celebrating the small wins. The small gains, like waking up in the morning... GREAT SUCCESS! It's a source of happiness and, therefore, a source of love. The small gains all connect and reinforce one another, like droplets of mercury attracted to one another to eventually create something massive.

LOVE AS A COMPETITIVE ADVANTAGE

Misery loves company. Guess what? So does love. And when we love together, it can become a competitive advantage.

Recalling my conversation with Tony Whatley on Joseph Jaffe is not Famous, we were discussing the curse of the silver-haired who tend to age out of the workforce by "someone half your age who will work twice as hard as you for half the pay." Younger workers today are very different from older workers from yesterday, but it's actually not true that someone half your age will work twice as hard as you for half the pay. The reality is they'll work half as hard as you and expect double the pay because of "The Great Resignation" and don't expect them to actually show up at your office. Also, don't mess with their pronouns.

THE RISE OF SILVER-HAIRED REVOLUTIONARIES

This is why the silver-haired revolutionaries will lead this next wave. Once the nest is empty, college has been paid for, the mortgage is in cruise control, and playing golf seven days a week has become a bit of a bore, people want to get back to work. They don't need as much. They already have the work ethic.

Perhaps our Gen Z and Alpha friends need to start conceding, **"there's someone twice our age who will work twice as hard for half the pay... holy crap, we had better get our act together."**

THE POWER OF LOVING WHAT YOU DO

Tony had a different take on this. *It's not that you have to love what you do, but if you don't, you're competing with someone who* ***does*** *love what they do... and that's not a fair fight. You've got no chance.*

So if you don't love what you do, you're stacking the odds against yourself. You are essentially self-sabotaging yourself by not being all-in and lovin' it. There are still people ("Splitters") who switch off their work phones and disconnect from email at 5pm on a Friday and resume at 9am on a Monday. They're doing themselves a disservice. They've compartmentalized their life and signaled that their job is not a part of their lifeforce. They live a split life. They have a fractured identity. Severance: Art imitates life.

CHAPTER 17 - AMOR

I know what you're thinking and so before you push back, I'll do it for you by making two points:

1. This is not a license for an employer or boss to take advantage of an employee by expecting them to be "always on" 24/7/365.
2. Corollary: you should be able to take breaks ("Blenders") during the 9-5, Monday to Friday and do "personal stuff." It has to cut both ways.

This is typically the life of an entrepreneur, small business owner, founder, creator, freelancer, or hustler anyway. Why can't it be the life of a salaried, W2 employee as well?

If your career, profession or job is not your lifeforce, maybe it should be. And if it isn't, maybe it's time to move on to the next question, although I can tell you the answer right now. If you're not doing what you were meant to do. This isn't your purpose. This isn't your calling.

You need to move on.

Discover what that calling is. I absolutely believe that anyone and everyone can and should love what they do, regardless of what it is.

DEATHBED CONFESSIONS

What do people say on their deathbed? What can we learn from people in their last moments?

"I should have spent more time in the office?" said no one on their deathbed ever! My argument for many years is that this is wrong. People should say, "I should have spent more time in the office." Of course, these days you don't actually have to physically spend more time in the office to have spent more time in the office especially when your office is 10 feet away from your bedroom! It's not about literal time or physical space.

Not if you merely went through the motions. You took the salary check. You punched in and punched out. It was rote. It was repetitive. It was monotonous. In which case, don't let the door hit you on the way out.

It means I could have done more while I was there. I could have been more productive. I could have been a better team player. I could have loved more or learned to love. Sometimes we learn to love through- and over time. Putting in the reps of love. It all fits together beautifully.

DYING WITH ABUNDANCE

When people say "I came from nothing" which is amazing to recognize the achievement of working your butt off and creating something substantial, they still need a reminder that when they are gone, they have returned to nothing.

All the money in the world still amounts to complete bankruptcy when all is said and "gone."

Some people are so poor, all they have is money – Bob Marley

This is why we want to have maxed out our relationship credit limit, which has a dollar value of 1 and an intangible value that is limitless.

Do you want it now or when I'm gone?

Without love, you can get by; you can survive. But if you want to thrive, you can only do it through love.

DO WE NEED A MATRIX TO WORK THIS OUT?

I'm sure there are people who don't love what they do and are happy. Just being grateful to have a job can be enough, but why not have both?

I don't think the opposite can be true, however. It's not possible to love what you do and not be happy.

EMBRACING GROWTH

There's a third variable that happily nuzzles and nestles within the love and happiness connection and it's not money; it's growth. Growth is both the alpha and the omega of a life well-lived and a life well-loved. It is the output, the outcome, and as it completes the cycle, the input to boot. When it becomes monotonous, staid and repetitive; when there's no freshness, the shine wears off, the collateral damage is the loss of love. You have to inject some spontaneity, the unexpected, to shake things up, mix things up, surprise and delight and yes, we're talking about work here.

Keep love alive.

The more we continuously and continually evolve, mature, and grow, the happier we'll be, the more fulfilled we'll be, the truer to ourselves we'll be. It is a virtuous cycle.

LOVE AND REGRET

On their deathbeds, people express a lot of regret. Dan Pink wrote about this in his book, "Regrets – How Looking Backwards Moves Us Forward." Not much forward movement, though, when it's your time to go.

Pink mentions how as you get older, your regrets move from regrets of action to regrets of inaction. *If only I had...*

The bucket list and all the things we wanted to do but didn't. Why?

The regret on your deathbed is the worst kind of regret because there's nothing you can do about it. The regrets we have right now are different. They are joyous regrets because they come with another "at bat." You get another chance and another shot. It's never strike three. Until it is. Time of Death.

Your life should be filled with regret until the very last moment when you have none at all because you did it all.

You should be maximizing, not minimizing or marginalizing opportunities for regret.

At his hospital bed just after he passed away; he had left his pen and papers on top of the little side table. The papers were on his passion, his Unified Field Theory. The evening before he died, Einstein was hard at work writing and scribbling his thoughts and workings on this theory. A little later he stated to his nurse, "...I think I will rest for a while" and he placed the items on the table.

It's an opportunity or a curse depending on how you deal with it, how you absorb, internalize, and grow from it. This is like three-dimensional chess here.

Instead of starting the week with the Monday Blues, enduring Humpday, and celebrating TGIF, let's shift our perspective, shall we? How about embracing TGIM—Thank God it's Monday? It's a simple mindset shift that can transform our approach to work.

LEAVE IT TO MALCOLM.

Malcolm Gladwell recently criticized the concept of working from home. He emotionally questioned, "What have you reduced your life to?" But I could ask the same question of those who were separated from their families for five days a week, enduring long commutes, only to be confined to a cubicle farm like caged mice in a scientific experiment. It's like a dystopian episode of Severance, with the memories being all too real and nightmarish.

Break rooms, finger traps, and waffle parties can never replace the joy of telling your child a bedtime story and tucking them in.

BORN TO BE HAPPY

Children are naturally happy. They are born happy. This is their natural state. They have to find a reason to be sad. Sadly, as they grow up, this reason is all too often their jobs. Adults on the other hand,

CHAPTER 17 - AMOR

have to find a reason to be happy. Perhaps the events of the last 3 years are the impetus or the reason for you to find that happiness.

There's still time. Until there isn't.

While discussing this book with a 94-year-old and his 89-year-old wife, I saw the regret and tears in his eyes as he recounted his three-hour daily commute over 26 years. The wasted years. The sheer waste.

Was this love? Was this life? Was this living? Or was this dying?

"Get busy living or get busy dying." – Andy Dufresne

CHAPTER 18
VERITAS

"Be yourself. Everyone else is already taken." – Oscar Wilde

IT'S NOT ENOUGH TO LOVE WHAT YOU DO.

Love can change. Circumstances will change. You will have no choice but to change as well.

What is needed and necessarily is a North Star to keep you on course; on track; forward focused.

Remember the essence of this message is to respond to the giant 2x4 that just whacked humanity across the face, and while it may never happen to all of us at the same time, the same way again, something most certainly will happen to you. It is inevitable. Just ask Thanos.

We need to love what we do AND be true to ourselves, but what does that truly mean?

CHAPTER 18 - VERITAS

One possible answer emerged when I asked my wife about the meaning of being true to oneself. She emphasized the idea of potential, and in particular, living up to it. In other words, being true to oneself involves realizing and maximizing one's potential, not wasting time or missing opportunities for personal growth and actualization.

At the end of the day, when the microphones are turned off, the lights are dimmed, the makeup is removed, and you face your unfiltered reflection in the mirror, what do you see? Who do you see? Look deep. Look deeper. Who is staring back at you? Do you genuinely love that person, or can you not look at them in the eyes?

As far as *that* day was concerned, do you feel like you lived it for yourself or for others? Was it driven by the need for external validation to fuel your ego? Did you require praise, recognition, and superficial gestures in order to fool yourself into a false sense of security and a reality distortion field of meaning?

HAS EVERYONE BEEN LYING TO YOU?

ARE YOU LYING TO YOUSELF?

I'm still competitive. I still don't want to finish last. That's why I filter my Peloton leaderboard to the 50+ category, so I can weed out the young bucks. It's okay to give yourself a little boost every now and then. After all, we're not machines. We need affirmation. But when we crave validation incessantly, it becomes an obsession, even an addiction. That's why so many celebrities are plagued by insecurity. And that's precisely why I am not famous.

I asked this question to Roberto Blake on my show: Why are celebrities so damn insecure? His response:

> *This is simple. Why would they be secure? Everything they have is predicated on other people's opinions. Think about it: if your entire identity is based on what others say about you, and your value*

is tied to making others feel good, your worth is contingent upon their beliefs and expectations. Your life is never truly owned by you; it's owned by others. Your identity, too, is not in your control but in the hands of others. While people may mourn the great singer or actor, the reality is that when you're in the ground or on your deathbed, nobody truly sees you, even if you have millions of fans. This insecurity arises from the fact that the world is in love with a facade, the best version of themselves, which is unsustainable. Any dent in their armor, any human mistake, can be harshly criticized and haunt them for years. Even past acceptable actions can come back to haunt them. They have to live with this anxiety every day, knowing that those who claim to love them can betray and turn on them, disregarding the life's work they've built without a second thought.

And when they are dead and buried, people will mourn the idea of them, not the individuals themselves. They will know that their death will be a lonely experience. While this may sound bleak and overly dramatic, I once read a book called "Legend" by my favorite author, David Gemmell. It portrayed a warrior named Druss the Legend, who, in his sixties, had survived every battle undefeated. He believed it was because his name and reputation preceded him, allowing him to win battles he shouldn't have. However, when he dies, everyone will mourn the legend, not the man. Nobody truly knows him as a human being. He has buried all his friends, his wife, his sons, and his warrior blood brothers. The only solace he has is the hope of embracing them again in the afterlife. He will leave behind no one who truly knew him as a man. He will only be mourned for the legends and stories told about him, leaving him with a profound sense of loneliness. This idea has stuck with me since my twenties. People may know of you, admire your fame and infamy, and construct a legend around you, but they don't genuinely love you. They love the story and the image they have in their heads. It's a sobering thought. Therefore, when discussing the

CHAPTER 18 - VERITAS

> *insecurity of celebrities, it is because everyone knows more about the legend than the person. No one mourns the man or woman because nobody truly knows them. How can anyone know them?*

As I have mentioned numerous times before, "be careful what you wish for" or, as AZ Benza put it, "Fame, ain't it a bitch?"

Living an anonymous life holds an extraordinary appeal. Leading a life where the only individuals who should genuinely care about you are not just yourself but also your loved ones.

CELEBRITY IN SENIORITY

Undoubtedly, the higher one climbs the ladder, the more complex it becomes. The social ladder. The corporate ladder. The celebrity ladder. And when this happens, we often lose a critical piece of ourselves, ourselves!

We're constantly proving ourselves. We have to be tough...strong...resolute. Can't show weakness. Can't reveal even the smallest crack in our impenetrable armor.

"At scale, cracks become chasms."

And the more we believe our own bullshit, the more we lose ourselves; the more lost we get. Enter "success theater" from the boardroom to the box office to the White House. Surround yourselves with yes men and women and you have a force field that shields you from the outside world; only you are its true prisoner.

THE DOUBT OF THE BENEFIT

COVID has changed many things in the world, but one of them is the way we think about vulnerability.

When I was laid off, I was deemed weak. I became damaged goods. Shortly before I was handed my pink slip, I had been interviewing with a media agency by the name of Universal McCann. They had been fawning at my feet and when I suddenly became a free agent, I gleefully called to let them know I was available.

They never called back.

At the time, I felt Universal McCann gave the company that laid me off the benefit of the doubt, but now I realize the doubt lay within me.

I doubted my worth. My value. My benefit.

Perhaps it really came down to one word: Truth.

I was not living my truth. I was not living my purpose. I was destined for something else.

I had another conversation with my wife about how our lives would have unfolded if I hadn't been laid off. What would our lives have looked like? Could I have become the CEO of Omnicom? Perhaps. Would we truly be happy? Perhaps not.

All the boxes would have been ticked, but that little voice in the back of my head might not have been entirely convinced.

How could the CEO of Omnicom be the host of a business talk show? Just saying.

In certain aspects of my life, I am a fatalist, especially when it comes to placing my faith in a higher power. Believing in a higher power gives me solace, knowing that I am not bewildered and alone. However, I also strongly believe in my ability to shape my own destiny. I understand that I am not a puppet controlled by some omnipotent master puppeteer in the sky. This realization also means that I am not shielded by that same higher power.

If there are no strings attached to the mannequin of my life, then it stands to reason that there are no safety nets beneath me either.

CHAPTER 18 - VERITAS

What if we are our own highest power, particularly when it comes to our daily lives? This is not to deny the existence of a greater force, but to recognize that, ultimately, we are responsible for our own journey.

Now, if you believe that everything happens for a reason, then you must also believe that this global pandemic occurred for a reason. Because if it didn't, that would be disheartening. It would make me feel unbearably alone to attribute the past several years to mere randomness or the actions of a clumsy human that changed the world. Forever.

So what's the reason? Could it be as simple as a message to each and every one of us to actualize and make Maslow proud?

I cannot control external circumstances. I can barely control myself. Every day, I struggle not only to be true to myself but also to remain true. If I am honest with myself, then I must also be honest with others, but above all, I must trust my intuition and not let the voice of doubt—self-doubt and self-sabotage—overwhelm me.

As I ponder this, I realize that there are multiple competing voices within me. And I recognize where I'm headed. When we find ourselves listening to numerous voices, it may be time to seek professional help or support. It's a complex journey to be true to ourselves, yet it's also a simple one.

Start by engaging in introspection each day. If this were your last day, would it have been a good day? Would it have been worth it? Would you have done what you did? Did you venture outside your comfort zone? Did you change someone's life? Did you make a difference? Did you take a step forward? Did you move closer to your goals?

Yes, it's a lot to contemplate. It places a significant burden on one person's shoulders. The solution is not to bear the entire weight alone but to share it with those who genuinely want to help, even if some of those people are strangers. This is the beauty of a caring community of strangers who extend their support beyond expectations. It's an incredible gift.

There's already enough pressure imposed on us by external forces, but often, we place even more pressure on ourselves. We set unrealistic performance expectations and raise the bar impossibly high. Every time we step onto the stage, spotlight, or even Zoom, we feel the need to be perfect. But why? Why do we feel compelled to perform on the social media stage? We don't always have to be the stars of the show. We don't have to play a role that disconnects us from our truth.

To be true to ourselves, we must strip away the filters, camera angles, lighting tricks, and retouching. Remember Lauren Griffiths? You may not know who she is, but I do. She got my attention, and I invited her on my show. She replaced her slick, professional LinkedIn headshot with an authentic quarantine photo—half-dried hair, no makeup, and a hoodie. The response was overwhelming. It resonated because it didn't just touch a nerve; it strummed on all of them; it touched hearts. It connected with thousands of women (and men) who were living the same truth. Or the same lie.

When you embrace your true self, it releases the pressure. It liberates you from unrealistic and unfair expectations.

The noises die down.

The voices go away.

The only thing that remains is peace.

Let me share the story of Enrique Camacho, a guest on my show. After retiring as a corporal in the US Army—the second highest position under General—he decided to start his own coffee company. While waiting for a loan, he drove for Uber during the peak of the pandemic. Out of 403 rides, only 3 passengers were interested in hearing his story. He held no grudge against them, understanding they simply wanted to get from point A to point B amidst widespread paranoia and anxiety. Moreover, they likely saw his name, Enrique Camacho, and assumed he was an immigrant who might not even speak English properly.

"When I was in the army, I aimed to be the best Corporal in the world. And when I became an Uber driver, my goal was to be the best Uber driver in the world."

I learnt more from him as an Uber driver than a Corporal.

Being true to yourself means embracing your morals, ethics, beliefs, and values. It means taking pride in your work and in who you are.

When you are true to yourself, you're not constantly comparing yourself to others, including your past self. You're not striving to break personal bests but instead committing to continuous improvement. And when you stumble, have a bad day, or face challenges, remember to forgive yourself. Show kindness to yourself.

BREAK THE STREAK

Social media has wreaked havoc on our sense of self-worth. Take the concept of streaks, something you may have noticed with your kids. They mindlessly swipe through Snapchat, obsessively trying to maintain streaks by snapping photos and aimlessly sticking out their tongues. But really, who cares about these streaks? Streaks are meant to end; even Cal Ripken Jr.'s record-breaking streak eventually came to a close. But setting streaks that are impossible to maintain only leads to a dopamine-fueled high, followed by a deep sense of disappointment or, worse, that can come from retirement from the endeavor.

FOREVER CHANGED

I think of one particular scene from Forrest Gump. When he decided to go on that run, and he ran and he ran and he ran. And hundreds of people just started running with him. And he ran across the country. And then one day he just stopped. And everyone stopped with him. They all waited for the next move. What was he going to do now? Why did he stop? Where was he going next?

And then he spoke. And they all listened with bated breath.

"I'm pretty tired, think I'll go home now."

It was time. It was just time to stop. It was time to change direction; change course; try something else.

This might be my favorite tweet that captures a similar thought:

We tried some shit. We learned some shit. Now we're trying some new shit.

Run insanely long, and then, for no particular reason, stop and move on.

It's just life. Keep going. Keep growing. Keep moving. Celebrating the journey as opposed to the destination.

CHAPTER 18 - VERITAS

Figure out who you are; who you were meant to be and along the way, love every single second of it.

THE JOENESS BROTHERS

At a mindfulness retreat called MindCamp, run by The Mindfix Group, I participated in an exercise called "Golden Gossip."

Here's how it worked: we formed groups of three. One person would share their dreams and aspirations, particularly about what they envisioned doing after MindCamp. After sharing, this individual would turn their back, allowing the other two to "gossip" about them as if it were months into the future at a social gathering.

In my case, I spoke of my ambitions: publishing my 6th book, and in doing so, changing how books are marketed. I also spoke about growing my show, and dreaming of it being picked up by CNBC. My ultimate goal was to emerge as an "overnight success," even if it took 52+ years to get there.

Turning my back, I listened. The two young women in my group, likely in their mid-20s, began speaking effusively about me, how I'd achieved my dreams and realized my future. *Hey, did you hear about Joe? He got his show picked up. It's so amazing. We knew he could do it.*

They even came up with something they called *Joeness* (not Jonas Brothers), but Joe-ness. *I tell you, there's something about him, his optimism and his joy and his vulnerability and his willingness to share...hard to put a finger on it; it's like a kind of Joe-ness. And you know what, we all have a little Joeness in us...*

I just smiled from ear to ear. It meant so much to me. And it made me feel like a million dollars.

I want to make you feel like a million dollars too.

You know what? **You** have a little Joeness in you too.

FOREVER CHANGED

You know what? **You** have your own unique incredible essence as well. Your **you-ness**. Your Veritas.

Guess what? I have a little of your you-ness in me too.

Now go and discover it.

AS I LAY ME DOWN TO SLEEP...
Ask yourself these 5 questions:

1. Did I show up today for myself?
2. Did I show up today for others?
3. Did I live today like it was my last day?
4. Did I live today like it was my only day?
5. Did I live today like it was my best day?

If the answer to any of these questions is no, then do something about it. Change it. Forever. And if you don't get it right, guess what? There's always tomorrow...

'To thine own self be true' - act 1 scene 3, Shakespeare's Hamlet

CHAPTER 19
VIGOR

THE STORY BELOW IS AN EXCERPT FROM NAPOLEON HILL'S classic, "Think and Grow Rich." It's a "golden" illustration of this very subject. (The last two sentences beg to be written down and memorized.)

Three Feet From Gold

by Napoleon Hill

One of the most common causes of failure is the habit of quitting when one is overtaken by temporary defeat. Every person is guilty of this mistake at one time or another.

An uncle of R. U. Darby was caught by the gold fever in the gold-rush days, and went west to DIG AND GROW RICH. He staked a claim and went to work with pick and shovel. The going was hard, but his lust for gold was definite.

FOREVER CHANGED

After weeks of labor, he was rewarded by the discovery of the shining ore.

The returns proved they had one of the richest mines in Colorado!

Down went the drills! Up went the hopes of Darby and Uncle! Then something happened! The vein of gold ore disappeared! They had come to the end of the rainbow, and the pot of gold was no longer there! They drilled on, desperately trying to pick up the vein again— all to no avail.

Finally, they decided to QUIT.

*They sold the machinery to a junk man for a few hundred dollars, and took the train back home. Some "junk" men are dumb, but not this one! He called in a mining engineer to look at the mine and do a little calculating. The engineer advised that the project had failed, because the owners were not familiar with "fault lines." His calculations showed that the vein would be found **just three feet from where the Darbys had stopped drilling**! That is exactly where it was found!*

The "junk" man took millions of dollars in ore from the mine, because he knew enough to seek expert counsel before giving up.

*Before success comes in any man's life, he is sure to meet with much temporary defeat, and, perhaps, some failure. When defeat overtakes a man, the easiest and most logical thing to do is to **quit**. That is exactly what the majority of men do. More than five hundred of the most successful men this country has ever known told the author their greatest success came just one step beyond the point at which defeat had overtaken them. **Failure is a trickster with a keen sense of irony and cunning. It takes great delight in tripping one when success is almost within reach.***

CHAPTER 19 - VIGOR

THE CONCEPT OF ENDURANCE

"The Long Game" is not about short-term results. It implies a bigger plan, a master plan, if you will. The concept, once again, of zooming out, being able to see the big picture. Being able to move beyond the minutia of tactics. Even beyond the realm of strategy, to what is certainly the highest order: vision, and mission, and purpose.

THE VISION AND MISSION

The best time to plant an oak tree was 20 years ago. The second-best time was March 2020. It was for me. The third best time is right now.

We all get stuck in these comparisons and comparative thinking, where we're constantly worried, anxious, in our own heads about missing the boat, about being too late, about timing.

You can't burn a boat you missed right?

The fear of missing out or FOMO is real. From a psychological standpoint, marketers and salespeople are banking on it. Act now, while stocks last, a timer counting down. Everything is built in to raise our levels of anxiety and more often than not make a decision or make a purchase based on fear. I'm pleased to say, Forever Changed has its own spin on this. From FOMO comes JOMO, the Joy of Missing Out, something that my friend Shira Lazar has built an entire project around. JOMO is all about being at peace with not always having to participate or feeling the urge to step in, to step up, to be involved in everything. Because when everything matters, nothing matters. I've taken that one step further and I coined the term JOMU, the *joy of messing up* - the beautiful chaos of making mistakes; failing, learning and then getting back to work; realizing that on our life's mission, our life's work, the ultimate project, we're going to mess up so many times. But if we keep in our minds, our hearts, our head, our soul, a bigger picture; if we can zoom out to see that bigger picture in our mind's eye, to visualize it, to manifest it, then we have the superpower or *superskill* to play the long game.

FOREVER CHANGED

You've seen so many elements of "slow and steady wins the race" already in the book. Let's not forget our dear friend the penguin. We need more thinking. We need more thought leadership on the long game. Corporations need it too. The Third of the Four Horsemen of the Corporate Apocalypse or *Corpapocalypse* (from Built to Suck), is being a public company and it comes with a CTD (corporate transmitted disease) of short-termitis, the purgatory of being trapped in and captured within another Groundhog Day, quarterly earnings. Is it any wonder that companies can't transform or struggle to move forward? It's not that they're solely trapped in the past; it's equally the challenge of being **trapped in the present** - the day-to-day; the tactics; the weeds; the vicious cycle of not seeing the wood for the trees but seeing the trees for the wood.

If we gave companies the goose that laid the golden egg, they'd slaughter it and cook it on the barbeque.

As a company, brand, or even as an individual, you kind of need to figure out a way to live in both worlds - think of it as two camera angles, with two different lenses. The day-to-day, the here and now, but also the bigger picture.

Now utilize that telephoto lens to zoom out, because if you don't, you will never be able to move forward.

I often say the following to my kids, and they roll their eyes as usual: *if you're not going to worry about it five years from now, don't waste more than the next five minutes worrying about it now.*

The statement is so true. And it is so relevant and so accurate. I believe it was Nir Eyal on Stephen Bartlett's Diary of a CEO podcast, who talked about *scheduling time to worry.* I love that. Instead of worrying constantly and debilitating yourself, hamstringing yourself with anxiety, with doubt, with fear, with paranoia, schedule time to worry, and then wallow in that worry. Immerse yourself, swim in it, surround yourself, embrace it – and then figure out a

CHAPTER 19 - VIGOR

solution. Compartmentalize it and move forward. This is what it is to play the long game. This is what it is to run a marathon as opposed to a sprint. Pace yourself. Back to our penguin, it's a combination of fast walks and slow jogs and sometimes downright pauses and even slower walks. And then, of course, right at the end, the moment of victory, the sprint. Why not have it all? Why not be a tortoise, a hare, a penguin, and every mashed-up version in between?

When I was starting my show, I was given the advice, *"if you're not going to commit to it for the next two years, give up right now."* It didn't dissuade or demotivate me; it liberated me, realizing that I had two years to figure it out. And when two years came and went, I still hadn't figured it out. So it was time for another two more.

I will continue to do this until I drop dead. I'm never giving up, I'm never quitting. I absolutely may have to change many things, maybe everything: the name, the length, the format, the positioning, but the dream? That will live forever.

Almost one year has passed from the time that I announced this project and began the process of writing the book. It took me almost an entire year to finish it. Along the way, plenty of fear and paranoia that someone would steal the idea of the first book in the world where readers get royalties. I should have given up a year ago. I should have given in to the voices of doubt, who would have convinced me I was a fool for thinking I could pull this off.

These are the tricks. This is the devil that messes with our minds.

The cognitive dissonance, procrastination and inertia that prevents you from getting in the game. Never even getting started in the first place. This is why the first step is always the hardest step. And it's also the most empowering step, the most gratifying step. The ability to get unstuck, to make that first move. To just do it, to begin to roll, to begin to move. To move forward, to move forward consistently, to move forward consistently in the right direction. To change direction. And to keep this up, rinse and repeat, building momentum, building muscle memory. That's the power of endurance.

And the thing about endurance is that it takes incredible discipline, incredible staying power, incredible resolve, determination, resilience, grit, all of the above. To build endurance, you've got to put in the work. You've got to do your time. You've got to do the reps. You've got to put in your 10,000 hours. You've got to get so damn good at what you do that eventually you're in cruise control.

THE POWER OF ENDURANCE

The long game is the right game. But it's also the hardest game because of all the distractions, because of all the curveballs and the uncontrollables that are thrown your way, because of all the pivots that will be required, and they will be required. Why? Because guess what? How do you even know you're going in the right direction?

And what if that right direction at the time was absolutely the way to go, but now, it isn't. Now, there's a different way. Now, there's a better way. Why would you dogmatically or stubbornly stay the course when the course has been corrected? By someone other than you. Or what if you are the one that makes that course correction?

There are so many nuances and beautiful aspects of endurance. But the one that comes to my mind is the quote mentioned earlier in the book: *"If I had known then what I know now, I wouldn't have gotten involved."* What does that even mean? Well, on the surface, the message there is to just do it, to get started, to go into something with almost blind faith, with the lack of knowledge but full of heart. The message is, sometimes the best way to get started is just to get started, not to overthink it.

And if you become too obsessed with the details, it truly will prove to be the devil. The message in that quote is the ultimate message for an entrepreneur or for someone who is on their journey to become forever changed.

CHAPTER 19 - VIGOR

Someone that's prepared to make the change. Someone that's prepared to jump before they're pushed, and they will be pushed. The message is to trust your gut. And realize that your lizard brain is designed to talk you out of it every single time because of the risks, because of the opportunity costs, because of the unknown, because of how easy it is to get to no (and how hard it is to get to yes.)

The thing about these fears and pain is that it's your fear, it's your pain, it's your story, it's your dream. It's nobody else's, and no one can ever take that away from you. All of these thoughts come racing into my brain, into my mind, and hopefully into yours. When you're playing the long game, when you are participating in the ultimate marathon, the marathon of life, the ultimate project, and sometimes that marathon isn't a marathon, it's an ultra-marathon. And sometimes it's an extreme ultra-marathon. In fact, it almost always is. You want to live a long life? That's the ultra-marathon. You want to live a good life? That's the extreme part. Don't worry, you got this.

Or do you want to live a boring life, an uninspiring life, a meaningless life, a purposeless life, a bland life, a vanilla life, a forgettable life?

If so, call an Uber.

If not, get out there and climb Mount Kilimanjaro. Ascend Everest. Literally. Figuratively. Take on the challenges that life has to offer. Not like Sisyphus. Like you. Like only you can do. There is no other way.

If I'd known then what I know now, I probably would have gotten involved one year prior.

> If I'd known then what I know now, I probably would have gotten involved one year prior.

You see, the beautiful thing about the things that you could have, should have, would have done a year ago is that in a year's time, someone's going to be exactly where you are right now, going through the same thought process. And most of the time, they won't take action. They'll be talked out of it. They'll talk themselves out of it. They won't move forward. And a year later, they'll be in the same place. And a year after that, in the same place. And before they know it, the moment, their lives, the project would have passed them by. In this case, the pandemic would have passed them by. Don't be that person.

Perhaps you've thought about these changes for a long time, perhaps a year ago you were thinking about these changes. You can't go back in time, you can't get started earlier, but you can get started now. Rest assured that in a year's time, you will be one year ahead of everyone else that hesitated today; that procrastinated but struggled to get going.

Get in the game and then stay in the game. Keep on tweaking, keep on pivoting, keep on adapting, evolving, never stand still, keep moving forward. Always be prepared to change course, stay open to advice, but also trust your gut. You have one life to live, so why not live it? Why not truly be alive?

Here are three keys to include in your forever changed playbook.

THREE KEYS TO SUCCESS

Time. You have time. If you aren't able to make the change today, if the Global Pandemic wasn't enough for you, if you've got unfinished business, if you're just not able to quit your job, however miserable you might be, it's okay. I understand. I respect your responsibilities, your obligations, as well as your fears. But start planning, plant the seeds, start training for the marathon.

CHAPTER 19 - VIGOR

Experience. You have the experience. You have your entire life's experiences. Don't discount your life's work, the battle scars and the wisdom; the grit and the tenacity. Don't feel lesser than you are, don't feel lesser than yourself. Don't feel like you're not good enough. You absolutely are. Or turning it on its head, the less experience you have, the better your chances of being successful because you'll go into whatever it is that you choose to go into not knowing what you might have known or would have known or will soon know in the future. Remember, "If I'd known then what I know now, I wouldn't have gotten involved." Well, that "then" is "now" for you. So trade on your naivete, on your innocence, on your inexperience, on your incompetence. But with all of that present, nobody can take away your energy, your passion, your drive, your heart, your will to succeed.

Community. You're not alone. You never were. You have so many people who love you, who care about you, who want you to succeed, who will "will" you to succeed; followers and friends; counterparts and competitors. Lovers and strangers.

Perhaps I'm a stranger to you. Perhaps I'll change your life. Perhaps I'm no longer a stranger to you. Perhaps you're no longer a stranger to me.

As you sit down, whatever road you choose to go down, remember the power of multitasking. Every morning when I run my virtual coffee in the Collective Cafe, I tell people, "I don't want you on stage. That's not what this is. I want you on the treadmill. I want you walking the dog. I want you getting the kids ready for school. I want you on your commute, to multitask, to kill two birds with one stone. I want to feed your soul while you're feeding your body or feeding your children for that matter." And if you are on that dog walk, on that run, just like I was when I listened to Jerry Seinfeld talking about zooming out, that's when you truly will feed your energy, replenish your energy, motivate yourself to take on the world by taking on yourself. And realizing the only thing holding you back is you.

Perhaps one day you won't be listening to me at all. Perhaps I'll be listening to you. Or perhaps you'll be listening to **you**, listening to yourself, collecting your thoughts; being comfortable with the greatest person in the entire world: yourself. Thinking, dreaming, imagining, creating, at peace, realizing that sure, there is a mountain to climb, there is a marathon ahead, but at the same time, with pride, with accomplishment, realizing how far you've come.

Love what you do, be true to yourself, and stay the course.

Don't give up. You've come too far. And however far you still have to travel, it's just going to be awesome because you are awesome.

CHAPTER 20
SLIPPAGE

Just like you should never say never, it's "never" a good idea to talk in absolutes—every, all, always, forever.

Forever is a long time. In fact, you might say it's an eternity.

To say, "I'm forever changed" is delusional at best and arrogant at worst. How can you say that? How do you know? Moreover, how do you avoid yourself from slipping back?

What about slipping back to our bad habits?

Never forget where you've come from. Never forget. Never forget where you were before March of 2020. Never forget where you were in March 2020. Keep reminding yourself where you are and how you got here. Don't lose focus on where you are heading. Endurance does not mean complacency.

It's an awfully big promise to have to keep or expectation to have to live up to.

When I became a talk show host, I became forever changed. But what if I stopped? What if a job came along? What if someone made me an offer I couldn't refuse? Am I no longer forever changed? Was I just temporarily changed? Doesn't roll off the tongue as easily now, does it?

Or what about saying, "I'll never work for a company again." Think about all the people who have left the corporate world to pursue their entrepreneurial dreams. So many of them end up back in the corporate world, whether due to failure OR success (being acquired).

Suddenly, never seems like a pretty good outcome.

FOREVER CHANGED

If the right company came along right now and offered me a huge salary, would I take it? I'd like to tell you the answer is no. I can tell you my wife would respond with a "hell yeah" even though I'd be in hell. It's been over 3 years chasing the talk show windmill, perhaps it's time to grow up.

When we look at the phrase "forever changed" and especially in the context of "never saying never" and reverting to BP (Before Pandemic), **perhaps we should be focusing more on the word "forever" than the word "changed."**

Why? Because "changed" is a moving target. Change is dynamic, not static. Change is not about a destination. Change is about a journey. Life is a journey. The minute we stop and stand still on the treadmill or conveyor belt of life, we shoot back - we fall back.

If we're not growing and moving forward, we are stagnating and falling back, and specifically falling back into our old ways and bad habits.

My biggest fear at the start of this pandemic was that people would not see the signs, they would not take the opportunity, and would revert back to their old ways.

Like road rage or these days, airline rage. Road rage in many respects is a microcosm of life. Driving along, minding your own business, and somebody enters your life in the most surprising and unexpected way. And you have absolutely no idea who they are, what's going on in their life, what pains they're going through, what challenges they're going through. Perhaps they just made an innocent mistake or perhaps you did, but now both of you are brought together in a potentially explosive situation and both of you are driving massive, powerful weapons. And these days probably additional weapons in the car.

CHAPTER 20 - SLIPPAGE

And so you have a binary choice in those moments: escalate or deescalate. The only dents or dings are to ego, and even in the event of a fender bender, it's just money or less so, if you have insurance.

Perspective. It's not the worst thing that's going to happen in your life unless you make it. And you're not going to be worrying about it in 5 years' time, unless you do something you're going to regret. Majorly.

AP – After Pandemic – how will you react and respond in the simple situation of inadvertently cutting off someone on the road? Did your old self get angry with people for seemingly no reason, with zero empathy whatsoever and no clue about what's going on in their life? What about your new self? Are you changed?

Whereas "forever" is the devil we don't know, "change" is the one we do. There's so much that has been written on the subject of change. It's not just a goalpost that continue to shift as we continue to change, adapt, and evolve, but one that we often slam into as we careen into what we thought was the destination, but turns out it was just a steppingstone. With no destination, we only have the journey to fall back on. We might as well enjoy the ride, right? And with it, the ability to check in with yourself.

How am I doing? Am I on target? Am I on course? Am I ahead? Am I behind? Do I need to course correct? Is there a better course to take?

SLIPPAGE

I think I saw the word "slippage" on rally.io, the now defunct home of my creator coin/cryptocurrency. The term refers to when you are processing a transaction like converting one cryptocurrency to another, and the time between requesting, and the miners initiating, and completing the trade on the blockchain. During this "lag," there's likely to be a change in the exchange rate where the final rate may vary from the original quote.

And so you have an allowance for an acceptable level of slippage or variance.

I think there's something much meatier to unpack here, namely the price of hesitation. The longer you take, the more likely you are to encounter slippage. Even if you don't believe you are hesitating, in a dynamic world, the pace we move at may not be fast enough. So we have to allow for slippage.

That's the key, allow for it. Don't get despondent about missing out on the perfect deal, especially if you allow for variance. "Buy low, sell high" in your dreams!

In statistics, research, or polling, we talk about a 95% probability, with a variance of 5% allowed for *slippage*.

So let's go with 5% slippage as an acceptable level. 5% that governs, "Fire now, Ready, Aim Later" or "start now, course correct later." 5% acceptable decisiveness wiggle room.

SLIPPAGE FOR DUMMIES

The best way for me to illustrate slippage is through something that has been a part of my life for as long as I can remember—my weight.

I very publicly undertook to lose 30 pounds in six months. I wish it were the first time, but it's been a constant yo-yo struggle of weight gain and weight loss. When I've lost the weight, I've sworn every single time that I will never slip = and put back the weight. I've even thrown out the fat clothes. Now I regret it.

How did it come to this? How did I slip back? In my defense, and I would hope you would grant me some slack or slacks, I did have open-heart surgery. The inactivity from being unable to exercise for six months took its toll. But it's still no excuse. I can attempt to shift the blame, but I have to step up and take responsibility as well.

I did. I lost most of the weight. And then I put it back on. I slipped. Again. I swore I wouldn't ever again. Now I'm just swearing.

I'm putting this into the book because at some point you'll read it and you'll see me and I'll either be in the process of losing the weight or on the off chance I look like an Adonis, don't worry, I'll be back to my larger self soon. Sigh.

It's clear to me that we need a particular set of skills that govern the leg of the journey that moves us from the status quo to transformation. I hope that would be this book. We ALSO need a different set of skills that help us stay where we are: the resolve to endure and stay the course - a set of skills to help us from falling back.

JUST NOTICEABLE DIFFERENCE

There's a concept in marketing called the "just noticeable difference." When we lose or gain a little weight every single day, it's not noticeable to us or the people around us who see us every day, but it all adds up. This is why someone who hasn't seen you in a while will tell you to your face how much weight you've lost, or if you've gained the weight, everyone else will be telling each other behind your back.

Perhaps the only truth teller will be your once baggy pants that are now skin-tight or your button popping.

Question: How did it come to this? How can I avoid this from happening again…next time?

Answer: Early warning signs

Just noticeable difference works for candy bars (when you see "now with 25% more," it's just the marketers returning the bar to its original size before they shaved off a little bit too much in order to cut costs and you *noticed* this time) and it works for weight (it's called a scale), but it can also work for your lifeforce and specifically how you feed it or starve it.

JOURNALING

Journaling with purpose presents a whole host of techniques to counter slippage. I heard about a technique where you assign a 1-10 rating at the end of every day that aligns with happiness, fulfillment, or just a simple rating to the day. Did it rock or did it suck? And this way, you can graph it and look back on it to identify and pinpoint specific moments and memories that contributed to your mental state. What did you achieve? How productive were you? What made that day so special? It's not dissimilar to a currency, stock, or a bond. Looking back allows us to look forward.

Note to self: Create a Forever Changed Journal with 3 key metrics: Amor, Veritas and Vigor.

It might also help us answer the question, "Why did we slip back?" Was it a lack of self-belief? Did we "FUD" ourselves? Or was one of our 3 pillars deficient?

If money can't buy happiness, and money can't buy friends (at least not real ones) and money can't buy health, what can money buy?

MONEY BUYS TIME.

Breathing room. Room to breathe. Room to grow. Room to apply the just noticeable difference to your personal journey. You can apply it like a superpower to build the muscle of grit: small, baby steps that allow you to pull forward over time. It's like the Push-up Challenge. Today, you barely complete one push up, but tomorrow you make it. And the next day 2, and the next day 3, and before you know it, you're competing on American Ninja Warrior.

CHAPTER 20 - SLIPPAGE

If this is true, what causes us to regress from Ninja Warrior to Flappy Tabby? Perhaps it's the absence of personal guidelines and guardrails. The ability to check yourself and, Jedi-like use the force to your advantage. Motivate yourself forwards with small victories that recognize and reward your baby steps, and on the other end of the continuum, don't be fooled and disillusioned by the small losses.

Having a plan in place helps. Even more so if it's a code. Like Dexter, the Serial Killer Good Guy. Your code of forever conduct should contain things that have to be non-negotiable. For me, it's the show. Offer me a full-time job, and if you want me to say yes, sweeten the deal by feeding, not starving the show. The show stays.

When you forget who you are and where you've come from; what got you from "there to here," you compromise yourself.

At the same time, your code of forever conduct should contain things that are equally negotiable. A degree of humility and therefore flexibility is equally important. Talking in absolutes is problematic. So too is the word "forever."

Don't expect an easy path to remain forever changed, forever. You'll need to fight really hard to stay forever changed. It might even be tougher without that Global Pandemic in your corner, but fear not, there will be a slew of additional crises. Along the way, you'll need to be reflective, introspective, realistic, honest, but I believe the formula I've put into place - love what you do, be true to yourself, and stay the course - ***will*** help prevent you from falling back.

So what happens when COVID is well and truly in the rearview mirror, a footnote in history and reference point to the next crisis? Moving on itself is inherently the early warning sign of slippage.

> Moving on itself is inherently the early warning sign of slippage.

Therapists might disagree. Can we ever truly move on from this? Not if we want to remain forever changed. It has – for better or worse – shaped us and made us who we are today. Perhaps we need to carry this with us not as a weight or a burden, but rather as a badge.

Never forget.

DON'T BE SO HARD ON YOURSELF.

There are going to be good and bad days, and on a daily graph this will present itself in the form of extreme spikes, but when you zoom out, your moving average may be the smooth line of progress, momentum and actualization. Just like looking at a minute-by-minute chart of your daily stock portfolio versus a zoomed out 5-year or all-time illustration.

Slipping back is part of life, if – and only if – it's temporary or short-lived. Forgiving ourselves, giving ourselves grace, and not being so hard on ourselves helps oodles.

An accountability partner or accountability community helps as well. Being part of a community where people really have your back and genuinely take pride and pleasure in your success, even celebrate it, is the proof of concept for "community capitalism" – governed by a flame, not a pie. Forget trying to get a bigger slice of the pie or even growing the pie, the new model is about light. When I light your flame, together our flames burn brighter. There is no jealousy when the outcome is not zero-sum. When you are part of a community, where people can be honest and tell you what they think and feel, that is a safe place and space for continuous growth and negligible slippage.

A community is only as strong as its weakest member and if you can create a culture where collaboration, support and reciprocity triumphs over defensiveness, push back, and politicking, you'll create a sense of vigilance that checks slippage at the door and keeps toxic positivity or intense negativity at bay.

CHANGE SUCKS

I glossed over the change part of "forever changed" because I've been in the business of change my whole life and there are a gazillion books written on it, but here's a refresher.

"Change happens when the pain of not changing is greater than the pain of changing." It's all about pain, and so often times, it's choosing the lesser of evils, unless of course you enjoy the pain (see: entrepreneur). And here's the thing, the pain in question is universal because we're all alike. We're all creatures of habit, and we all love our daily routines, which implies NO CHANGE.

And we all went through the same global pandemic. Did you forget already?

We drive the same way to work (these days, it's a short commute from my bedroom to my office), go to the same Starbucks and order the same triple foam, non-decaf, soy vanilla latte (these days, I just press the button on my Nespresso for my Intensio).

You too? Don't worry, you're not alone. We're not built to change. The brain is a change resistor. It looks at stimuli and says, "where have I seen that before?" and then attempts to compartmentalize by putting those round pegs in round holes and square pegs in square holes. "Oh, that's fire. Fire is bad - fire burns. Stay away from that." So we almost have to fool the brain to feel again; train the brain to allow us to introduce new stimuli, rubric, or possibilities. Or other times, just ignore the brain completely.

Think with your heart.

I've been in the change business my whole life, but until this very moment, I've never considered and built slippage into the concept of change, and with it, a recognition or even concession that change is not a continuously progressive process. It's more about two steps forward, one step back; three steps forward, three steps back; zero steps forward, one step back; one step to the side, one step diagonally.

That's change. Literally. And when you add it all up, as long as the "net" change is positive, you are moving forward and THAT is a victory.

Moving is great. It's a lot better than atrophy. Or apathy. No one wants to be debilitated and hamstrung with fear. Making progress is even better, as opposed to walking around in a circle – flywheels are better than hamster wheels.

It's frustrating and it's awesome. It's painful and it's glorious. Just like exercise, it involves tearing the muscle of conformity, complacency, and status quo to build it back tougher, stronger, and more resilient. But if you love the process, or at least if you can tolerate it; if you can embrace it, you're in such a good position. And it's probably the same reason why you feel so good afterwards, especially when you've worked so hard.

These are the endorphins of change. These are the remedies to slippage.

CHAPTER 21
BLACKJACK

THE FINAL FINAL WORD

YOU'VE MADE IT TO THE END OF THE BOOK, BUT I THINK YOU know this is actually just the beginning. Maybe you're already on your journey and this was just a pit-stop along the way. Or perhaps you've arrived at your destination (congratulations!) Only it's just the end of one leg of a much larger adventure. The adventure of life.

I commissioned the image below on the freelance site Fiverr. It was a build and slight modification on something I'd seen before, but it was missing one step on the continuum. Would you believe the step missing was the penultimate one, "I'm doing it!"

The Stages of Forever Changed

I want you to know that no matter where you are on this continuum, it's ok. And it's not too late. And there's still time. There's always time.

Perhaps you'll journal every day or at a minimum, just keep a spreadsheet and indicate where you are on this continuum.

TIME TO PLANT YOUR OAK TREE

The seed of your oak tree is your story.

While I know that my story is the most interesting and meaningful story in the world, I also know that yours is too – in fact it is the most incredible story in the world because it is **your** story. Which is why I'll tell you again (like I did at the beginning of this book) to go and tell your story.

The story of your becoming. Who are you becoming?

Here's your narrative arc:

BP (Life before March 2020)

AP (Life after March 2020)

Your Forever Changed Statement

X Mark the Spot

Here Lies [   ]

As you recall the full impact of March 2020 and where you were when the world shut down, how you were impacted, and how you coped, you'll want to document everything - the sights, sounds, tastes, smells, touches, emotions, fears and more.

MY FOREVER CHANGED STATEMENT

Next, write down your *Forever Changed Statement*. Perhaps it'll read as a Manifesto. Here's mine:

[Statement beginning]

What is the outcome? Getting unstuck.

CHAPTER 21 - BLACKJACK

What is the problem? People that are stuck.

What does it mean? They're stuck, stuck in life, in love, in business. They are unable to move at all, unable to move forward, unable to figure out what to do at all. Figure out what to do first. Figure out what to do next.

These are people that are frustrated. Wouldn't you be? They're not happy, not fulfilled, not actualized. They may very well have a high-paying job, all the status and all the money in the world, but they're miserable inside. They're not doing what they love, not loving what they do. They haven't figured out their purpose, their why, their calling. In many respects, they're living for other people, not for themselves.

Now, we're not talking about cashing it all in to go and live on a farm in Peru. This isn't about a midlife crisis. It also has nothing to do with midlife; it can be any time in your life. When you're early on in your career, you don't know what you don't know. Everybody's telling you what to do, telling you to go through the motions, to paint by numbers, to focus on the playbook, to go to college, to go to grad school, to rack up all that college debt just to be able to play the game.

But the game is broken, the business model of life is broken, the game of life is broken. It favors the few, a select few players that are pulling all the strings, and that is not how life should work.

And when you're too old? You've aged out. Life has passed you by. It's time to start winding down old-timer. Nonsense!

Whether you were cruising or ghosting through life - dialing it in and going through the motions – the conveyor belt of life just continued to whisk you away, without any ability for you to change the speed, incline or just hit the pause button. To pause. To reflect. To introspect on whether you were living your authentic self; living the best version of yourself; on a timeline that was on your terms; not forced, faked, contrived or artificial.

To have peace of mind; to wake up every morning and jump out of bed; to not have to toss and turn and be up all night, filled with anxiety, anguish, fear, doubt, self-doubt, head trash.

That is what it means to get unstuck.

If you're unhealthy, the outcome is to become healthy. If you're unhappy in your marriage, the outcome is to be happy in your marriage. But to what end? You want to be healthy so that you can live a good life and a long life. You want to have a healthy marriage so that you can be happy, it's happiness with your soulmate. You want a soulmate, you want a best friend, it's more than just a happy marriage. It's a happy marriage with…

To be unstuck means to be able to move freely about your life. It means emotional mobility, psychological freedom. It means being untaxed and unencumbered. It means living in a world of inner and self-confidence, as opposed to lack of confidence or self-doubt. There's no imposter syndrome, because you're not an imposter. You're on a journey, and that journey is not an aimless journey; it's a focused, directed journey because you're ultimately doing what you love in every aspect of what you do.

Life is hard; life is not meant to be easy. No one said it had to be easy. No one said it was about everything just falling into your lap. No pain, no gain makes a lot of sense, but why does there have to be pain at all? Working hard and being fulfilled is to look back with pride and say, *"I did this, I made this, I created this. It wasn't easy, but it was worth it. I put in the hours, I put in the reps, I put in the time, I put in the blood, sweat, and tears. But at every twist and turn, I was happy. There was a smile on my face; I was doing what I was put on this planet to do."*

CHAPTER 21 - BLACKJACK

What were you put on this planet for? What is your purpose? What is your cause? What is your legacy? What will you leave behind? What will you have changed forever? For the better, for the betterment of the people around you, for the betterment of this world? Is that too lofty? Is that unrealistic? I don't think so. Listen, we're not talking about curing cancer; some people will. But you can do something ever so small and leave your mark. It could come from teaching. One life, one life that you changed. Somebody that comes back to you 20, 30, 40 years from now and cites a moment in class that you've long forgotten, but they didn't. They never forgot it. It changed their life. It changed the course of their life.

I've had that experience myself, where people have come up to me after a Keynote or days or weeks or months later saying that they changed their entire career for the better, never for the worse, because of my speech or my keynote. Sometimes we don't even get to know immediately the impact of what we do and how we do it.

So, I'm going to ask you this question: *what is the potential of someone coming to you 20 years down the line, down the road, and talking to you about a moment, a day, an interaction, an encounter, an experience where you literally changed their lives forever, for the better?*

That is what it is to get unstuck.

When I look back on the Global Pandemic, I think about the millions of people who lost their lives. Did they live their best lives?

And what about the people that survived? Are they living the best version of their lives? Are you? Are they alive? Are they truly alive? Or are they dead inside? Are you dead inside?

These are questions that I'm not afraid to ask. These are questions I'm not afraid to answer. These are questions I want you to be able to answer.

FOREVER CHANGED

I'm not asking you to have a Jerry Maguire moment. I'm not asking you to throw all caution to the wind. I'm not asking you to burn the boats. I'm just asking you to be true to yourself. I want you to be happy, and I need you to put a plan in place that can get you to where you need to get to, if not now, tomorrow, or the next day, or the next week, or even in 10- or 15-years' time, it's okay.

At the same mindfulness retreat, I was desperate to cram in one last session with one facilitator that everyone was talking about. Out of the corner of my eye, I kept on seeing her, kept on walking past, wanting to spend time with her but never finding the opportunity. She seemed to be spending so much time with everyone else because she was all in, and they were all in. And then time ran out. I tried to force it in; that one more moment, that one moment more. But it just wasn't there. And in the briefest of exchanges with her, I said, *"I feel like there's unfinished business and I need to spend a few minutes with you. I'm so close to the line. Just one more push and I can get over the line."* And she looked at me and said, *"What line? Where's the line? Who decided what the line was, where it was, or how close you were to the line or what you needed to get over the line?"* And I looked at her and said, *"you've basically given me what I needed."*

The goals, the objectives, the metrics, the measures, the measurements of what we consider to be success or successful, they're subjective, self-imposed, even arbitrary. They're dictated by others, by society, by norms, by conventions that are not necessarily our conventions. They may be right for others, but they may not be right for us. We end up living in a house that is too big for us. We end up living in a house that other people perhaps feel we should be living in, but maybe not the right fit, not the right one for ourselves, and what happens? When you realize you've been living above or beyond your means, where are those people now? Where are the people who gave you the accolades, the adoration, the validation? They're nowhere to be found. In fact, they're the ones talking about you now behind

CHAPTER 21 - BLACKJACK

your back. Was it worth it? Don't be tethered to anyone else's expectations of who you are, of who you are becoming, of what you should be, of how fast you should be moving, of anything that determines ultimately and feeds your life force.

When you are stuck, you have limited mobility. You might be moving all right, but are you actually getting anyway? Making progress? You're treading water, while taking water.

When you are unstuck, you're able to move in any direction, at your pace, at your speed, at your cadence. It's not just your feet; it's also your mind. It's your ability to think and to act freely.

Every step is a considered step. Every word is a considered word. You're not talking for the sake of talking. You're not moving for the sake of moving. You feel the strength of your convictions and the conviction of your confidence, born and anchored in identity, in purpose, in authenticity. That's what it is to be unstuck, to be living. You're living, you're alive. Every day is a new day. Every day is an adventure. Every day is your best day because it is filled with wonder and limitless possibility. Every day you are making progress. Forward progress. Generating momentum. Returning to growth.

Maturation, not just Market Share.

Perspective, not just Profits

Progress, not Perfection.

Growing up.

Growing into yourself.

Growing towards your Changed self. Forever.

[statement end]

X MARKS THE SPOT

Next, you'll want to determine where you are on the continuum between "I won't do it" and "yes, I did it." Identify your current state and recognize it is not static. It is dynamic. You may fall back - slippage (hopefully not); you may stay the same (hopefully not); you may make plenty more gains (hopefully)

The key is to begin to tell your story, then share your story if you're comfortable, and don't forget to keep updating your story, because it continues as long as you do.

My X marks the spot: Somewhere between **I will do it** and **I'm doing it!**

Here lies... [   ][2]

While you're at it, go and write your epitaph. Your eulogy. Your tombstone engraving.

What would it say if it was today? What would you like it to say?

Here's mine: *Here lies Joseph Jaffe. He sat on his fat ass watching football, chugging beer and eating chicken wings.*

I think not.

Here lies Joseph Jaffe. He helped people get unstuck, return to growth and become forever changed.

When I was 17, I read a quote that went something like this, *"if you live each day as if it was your last, someday you'll most certainly be right."*

It made quite the impression on me.

In many religions, confession is the ultimate final act of your elaborate project called life. You're supposed to do it right before you die,

---

2 Insert your name here

CHAPTER 21 - BLACKJACK

but here's the tricky part: how do you know when today is the day you're going to expire? The answer is surprisingly simple: you do it every single day.

Remembering that I'll be dead soon is the most important tool I've ever encountered to help me make the big choices in life. Because almost everything, all external expectations, all pride, all fear of embarrassment or failure. These things just fall away in the face of death, leaving only what is truly important. Remembering that you are going to die is the best way I know to avoid the trap of thinking you have something to lose. You are already naked, there is no reason not to follow your heart.

Yeah that wasn't me. It was Steve Jobs addressing Stanford's 2005 graduating class. I appreciate it if you thought it was though.

He also said this in the same speech:

I'm pretty sure none of this would have happened if I hadn't been fired from Apple. It was awful tasting medicine. But I guess the patient needed it.

Sometimes life's gonna hit you in the head with a brick. Don't lose faith. I'm convinced that the only thing that kept me going was that I loved what I did.

You've got to find what you love. And that is as true for work as it is for your lovers. Your work is going to fill a large part of your life.

And the only way to be truly satisfied is to do what you believe is great work. And the only way to do great work is to love what you do.

If you haven't found it yet, keep looking and don't settle. As with all matters of the heart, you'll know when you find it. And like any great relationship, it just gets better and better as the years roll on.

So keep looking. Don't settle.

FOREVER CHANGED

I'm forever grateful to Jobs for this speech. I even "think different" about Steve Jobs after watching it. You can watch here: bit.ly/Steve-JobsForeverChanged. Please take the time to take in the reactions of everyone, including – but not limited to – the students in the audience. Entitled? Nervous? Awkward? Ungrateful? Innocent? Do you think any of them appreciated that moment as it was unfolding? How much humility does a graduate from Stanford have at the time? Do they have any idea of what lies ahead?

Did you have any idea of what lay ahead of you on March 11th, 2020 (or thereabouts)

You're not alone.

Plenty of people did not get the chance to confess. They did not get to live their last day like it was their only day. They did not get to embark on the journey to become forever changed.

You are different though. You are special. You have everything to live for.

Starting now, the first Tuesday of every month in the Collective Cafe (get directions to the cafe at foreverchanged.life) will be Forever Changed Tuesdays. It's an opportunity for YOU to join us and tell your story or hear others' stories. Share your Forever Changed Statement. We'll pour positivity into you until you overflow. It's an opportunity to support one another and collectively move through the continuum.

We can do it. Together.

THE CONTINUING JOURNEY

You've reached the end of the book. And if you think my story is complete, you would be wrong. If my story was complete, my life would be complete. And if my life was complete, well, I wouldn't be here anymore, writing this book or talking to you now, would I? Is there a happy ending to my story? Perhaps, perhaps not. Will I ever become famous? I'm sorry. What I meant was, "will I ever become 'not famous'?" I guess I already am, so mission accomplished.

In all seriousness, my story is a work in progress. My progress is incomplete. It's all part of my journey. And while I might not put pen to paper and document my progress in another book or the next book, all you have to do is reach out to me or Google me and find out how I'm doing. Just like I can do the same thing for you. And I will.

THE IMPORTANCE OF REACHING OUT

One of the most important things to do is to reach out to someone. Someone random, someone close, someone estranged, on a fairly regular basis and just check in with them. "Hey, I just wanted to see how you're doing." I remember doing an episode of my show, and it really struck me when one of my guests spoke about how he absolutely abhorred the words "hope all is well," as a throwaway greeting that we all use when we write emails. "Dear John, hope all is well... Anyway, about the thing that I was trying to sell to you..." What he does now is he replaces it with something along the lines of "Hope all is well, and if it isn't, please let me know what I can do for you." Reach out to people who may appear to be happy and content on the outside, as indicated by their perfect life on Facebook or their filtered life on Instagram, but inside, they might be struggling; they might be hurting. They might be looking for a reason to give up. And you, my friends, are the reason they won't. The ability to remind them to keep going, to remind them that life is a project, to remind them about the journey versus the destination. And quite frankly, to remind them that we're all in the same boat.

Remember that clichéd line from the pandemic, "We're all in this together." Except we weren't. Except we are. Except we can choose to live that line as a mantra, as a North Star, as a badge of honor. Because we are all in this together. And by this, of course, I'm referring to life itself.

And life is worth living, and life is worth loving. And when we see the signs and when we get our priorities in place and when we live aspirationally to the point where when we die, we have only one dollar to our name – literally or figuratively – you decide. You get to choose how you live your life; you get to write your story, even if it involves a ghost writer or AI chat bot.

DEFINING SUCCESS AND LEAVING A LEGACY

All of these ideas in the book center around the same simple premise: tell your story, live your story, celebrate your story, and celebrate other people's stories.

Love what you do, be true to yourself. Stay the course.

Do your best. Do your best at all times, do your best in general.

Push yourself and try not to get pushed when the next crisis comes along (and it will), but remember a forced change is still better than no change at all.

Or, you can spot the early warning signs, plant and sow the seeds of change on your own steam, on your own terms.

You could also jump. Take the leap. Take the plunge even if it appears to be a cold plunge. Your leap could be a leap of faith, but have faith in the fact you are not alone. And when you do, leap forward, leap ahead; leap with joy. Take a chance. Make a change. Be the change. Forever change.

Forever changed.

ABOUT THE AUTHOR

Joseph Jaffe is Natalie Jaffe's son.

This is his 6th book and his best one yet. Everything in his life has been leading up to this.

His previous books include Life after the 30-second spot, Join the Conversation, Flip the Funnel, Z.E.R.O. and Built to Suck.

As a teacher, facilitator and coach, Joseph helps high-aspiring entrepreneurs, business owners, and their leadership teams get unstuck, return to growth, and become forever changed. He does this as a Professional EOS Implementer® at EOS Worldwide (eosworldwide.com/joseph-jaffe).

He is the creator, showrunner and host of business talk show "Joseph Jaffe is not Famous." (youtube.com/josephjaffeisnotfamous and subscribe at bit.ly/subscribetotheshow)

He shares his knowledge and experiences via his Substack (jaffejuice.substack.com) and weekday virtual coffees in the Collective Cafe (directions at foreverchanged.life)

Jaffe is @jaffejuice on all the major socials.

For all additional links, please visit foreverchanged.life and linktr.ee/jaffejuice

www.ingramcontent.com/pod-product-compliance
Lightning Source LLC
Chambersburg PA
CBHW050334010526
44119CB00004B/140